The buzz about *Eclectically Criminal*:

"A superbly crafted collection of suspense and thriller shorts, marinated with deliciously unsavory characters and compelling plots that examine the criminal mind. Enjoy in a well lit room - and do your best to ignore the curious thump from the darkened hallway." Janice D'Agostino, Spoon Mage™

"Eclectically Criminal: Eclectic Writings Volume 2 presents a gripping, and sometimes disturbing, journey through a diverse landscape of criminal vignettes." Jody Carlson, avid reader

"My favorites from this amazing collection of crime stories are The Pit and The Silencer. Great suspense and sweet twists!" Laurence Levine, avid reader

"This collection takes the reader on a rollercoaster ride of emotions, from the hilarious bank robbery gone wrong of the Barré brothers to the gripping pain of a young girl's rape. 'Wow!' was all I could say at the end of this great volume." Elvia Valeria, CPA

Other Inklings Books

These great books are available at amazon.com

Anthologies:
Eclectically Carnal Volume 1 of the Eclectic Writings Series

Novels:
Payback by Ramon del Villar – book one in the Roberto Duran series

Nonfiction:
An Interpreter's Anatomy of a Civil Lawsuit by Ramon del Villar

Coming in 2015:
The Assassin by Ramon Del Villar – book two in the Roberto Duran Series

Eclectically Vegas, Baby! Volume 3 in the Eclectic Writing Series

Smiley Face Blatoon by Lady Nefari Ydarb of planet Jorn

Eclectically Criminal
Eclectic Writing Series
Vol. 2

Edited by

Fern Brady

Inklings
Publishing

www.inklingspublishing.com

First U.S. Edition

Edited by Fern Brady

Editorial Services, Johnnie Bernhard 808-227-0682

Cover Art by Eugene Rijn Saratorio

Eclectic Writings Vol. 2

ISBN: 978-0-9910211-2-3 by Inklings Publishing
http://inklingspublishing.com

Dedication

This volume is dedicated to Enos Russell, whose support,
encouragement, and knowledge have been invaluable.
Thank you my friend.

Table of Contents

The Silencer

by

Melissa Diane Algood

The Silencer
by Melissa Diane Algood

I popped the cork on the Cabernet, cut into the steak a dead woman grilled, and pondered the situation.

I remembered what it felt like to have them tear through my house several months ago. Our couch was flipped over, laundry removed, and the basement destroyed. We'd just had it remodeled for what would one day be a growing family, but they didn't care. A dozen men in uniform thoughtlessly busted through the walls of my home with sledgehammers. My jewelry, clothing, even a blender were boxed up, and labeled.

"Those are gifts," I told them as they wheeled my life out the front door.

Their faces were void of emotion as they stacked the life Kyle and I had made into the back of a police car. Our marriage became nothing more than words on a crumpled piece of paper shoved in a file.

> *It's from his victims, they told me.*
> *It's stolen property, they told me.*
> *None of it was ever yours, they told me.*

What they didn't know is my husband couldn't end a life. As an acclaimed psychiatrist, Kyle would take his patients' calls day or night, even on our third anniversary. Kyle had reserved a five star hotel for the night, but a suicidal nursing student called, and he was gone before he saw my new lingerie.

11

A gentle man, he would scoop up a spider in his open palm and gently set it outside, far from any predators, like our tabby cat, Lion. I should have asked the cops to take Lion too because, ever since they took Kyle, our four legged, furry child has howled for him. Maybe Lion didn't think I'd cried enough when they handcuffed Kyle in our front lawn on his way to get the paper.

The neighbors saw his car, they told me.
We found blood staining your upholstery, they told me.
We know he took that route home from work every day, they told me.

For days Lion howled. After the arraignment, and that outrageous Judge denying bail, I had to leave. I only got as far as the retro diner in the center of town, but I just had to get away from the sound of my cat's sorrow. I pointed to a glossy picture on the menu, and a young waitress placed a burger and fries in front of me. Ketchup, that I dipped my fries in, was really blood that ran like stripes up the walls and across the ceiling.

The next day a fake smile from a soccer mom at the grocery store reminded me of the teeth that were yanked out of every victim's mouth, postmortem. By weeks end, giggling, witty banter, and singing at the hair salon caught me off guard, as well. It was because all the victims' voice boxes had been removed while they were still alive, the reason the killer was dubbed 'The Silencer'. It wasn't clever enough to illicit an eye roll from me.

Everything reminded me of what Kyle 'did'. When I walked through town, to pick up my prescriptions, ladies crossed the street when they saw me coming. The story I heard them gossip about, while I waited in line behind them at the bank, wasn't close to the truth. They didn't know.

During my first police interview, I didn't need to see the crime scene photos for images of torture to fill my mind. The eventual release engulfed me. Besides, the cops wouldn't let me view them, no matter how often I asked.

"How could you not notice your husband gone?" asked a cop I thought looked too young to grow facial hair, much less carry a gun. My whole life went to hell because of that kid cop.

"He'd leave all the time for his patients."

"Where to?" The cop's pen danced across the page of the notebook he retrieved from his coat pocket.

"Hospitals, businesses, rooftops," I shrugged. "Wherever people feel suicidal, it's not as if he could be very specific. He's a medical professional."

"He'd just leave and never check in?"

"He called me every night at eight. It was our rule, no matter where we were, we called each other." It all seemed so stupid now, especially since we'd never get to do that again. "There's no way he did what you're saying."

The officer sighed. "People like this have a sickness. They're able to hide in plain sight."

"You're telling me my husband killed six families over the past two years and he kept it from me? He couldn't keep the end of a movie a secret if he saw it before me."

"So, do you know something about the murders?"

"No!"

The kid cop smiled, "I thought you didn't have any secrets?"

"Everyone has secrets." I realized too late that my words were dark, like tinted glass.

"Then you don't know..."

"I know Kyle is innocent!" The growl came from the depths of my gut. "I know he had nothing to do with this!"

His dark eyes brushed the Spanish tile of the floor. "You didn't question all the money coming in? Or why he had to remodel so quickly?"

I huffed, wishing I had a bottle of wine to go along with the questions. "It was my idea to remodel, and he wanted it done quickly, because I was pregnant."

The pen halted, and kid cop raised an eyebrow. "Was?"

"Was."

"What happened?"

I sighed. "I'm broken."

The cop started up again, but I had a question of my own, "Since you refuse to give me back my husband, when can I have the car?"

"As soon as we're done with our investigation."

"Soon?"

He shook his head, and that's when I knew I'd never see Kyle again.

He'd never rent some terrible horror movie and force me to watch it, or bring me my favorite flowers on my birthday, or refuse to separate the sheets from his blue jeans when doing the laundry.

Obviously, you're better off, friends said.
It's not your fault, co-workers said.
In time you'll heal sweetie, my parents said.

They never gave back the car Kyle bought me, which forced me to buy a new one. My new sedan was dark blue, which the dealer recommended for safety. I wanted to tell him that airbags couldn't keep me safe from a serial killer spouse, but I refrained myself and handed him the asking price in cash. Kyle was gone, so I figured I should go as well. Lion would find new owners, better owners. I got in the driver's seat, typed the address into the GPS, and drove.

Then I sat in my new car and waited.

From the heated leather seats, I watched the Nelsons eat dinner. A pumpkin stood next to their front door, a jagged carving of a witch faced me. It would rot in three days' time along with the perfect family of four. There was thirtysomething Donna with her long blonde hair and beauty queen smile spooning mashed potatoes onto each of the four plates. Brian was equally as aesthetically pleasing. He lightly caressed Donna's hand at the end of the meal, while the kids cleared the table for dessert. The twins Mia and Megan, were replicas of their mother: blue eyes, curly light hair, dimples, and long slender necks. Tonight the girls wore matching pale pink dresses with embroidered roses on the seams. Donna brought a pineapple upside down cake from the kitchen to the table for Brian to cut. She set the knife in the sink afterwards, just a few feet from the door I knew was unlocked.

I counted to one thousand once the house went dark. Before I walked in, I disabled the phones and internet using some gadget the nerd at the local electronic store told me was the best. I relished the forty paces to the carpeted stairway, then made a left into the twins' room.

It looked as if someone had poured Pepto-Bismol over every square inch of it. I stood over Mia first, watched her chest rise and fall with her slow, deep breaths. Her cheeks were flushed and her eyelashes lightly fluttered before I put a pillow over her face to muffle her screams as I suffocated her. The same fate came to Megan, before I took the pliers from my utility belt and removed their teeth. Most of their mouths were filled with baby teeth. Those I tucked into my pocket.

The parents were always a challenge. Brian had his arm wrapped around Donna which made it easier for me to hold a rag over each of their mouths. The mothers were always easy and quick, almost too quick. But, I loathed Donna. She had everything I wanted. Everything. I got a little overzealous with the pliers, and unhinged her jaw from her skull.

Brian was more difficult, because his eyes were the same chocolate color as Kyle's. It was as if my husband were looking up at me, pleading.

"I'm so sorry, baby." I cooed in Brian's ear as I dug through his glottis and snipped his vocal chords. "I wish you were here to watch me, like before."

After Brian's eyes lost their vigor, I strolled back into the dining room, and poured myself a glass of Robert Mondavi. While their bodies chilled above me, I sat at the table, and scavenged on the leftovers of their dinner that Donna had so artfully placed in Tupperware. The steak was still juicy, as if she'd just taken it off the grill. It was long past eight, and

16

Kyle couldn't get to his cellphone, the police had it in evidence, but I made the call anyway. After four brief rings, it went to voicemail.

"You've reached Dr. Kyle Whitmore. If this is an emergency, please hang up and call 911. If not, then please leave me a detailed message, and I'll get back to you shortly."

"Hey, it's me. I just wanted you to know that I love you, I really do. I know you think people like me don't feel human emotion, but we do, sometimes. Don't blame yourself, Kyle. I never meant for you to get hurt, not you of all people." I didn't know what else to say, so I hung up, and took my husband's advice.

"911, What is your emergency?"

"I'm Jessa Whitmore. The Silencer."

The Great Louisiana Bank Robbery

by

Thomas Mitchell

The Great Louisiana Bank Robbery
by Thomas Mitchell

The engine coughed and sputtered, and the old truck rolled to a stop.

"Dammit. Outa gas again." Clyde Barré pounded his fists on the steering wheel. "I thought you put some in last night," he said to his brother, Bobby.

"I don't have any money."

"We never have any money. Ain't no jobs way out here in the country. Not even any farm work."

"We need some cash. Maybe we could rob a bank," Bobby said.

"Yeah, sure. But right now we gotta find somebody to tow us to Jesse's."

In the spring of 1934, Jesse LeBeau owned the only filling station in the isolated rural community of Levee, Louisiana.

"Who do we know that lives close by?" Bobby asked.

The chug, chug, chug of a tractor answered him. "It's Mr. Doucet," Clyde said. "I bet he'll give us a tow."

Alcide Doucet stopped his ancient Fordson tractor when he saw the Barré brothers. "What's the matter boys?" he asked.

"Outta gas," Bobby said. "Reckon you could tow us to Jesse's?"

"I s'pose. You got a chain?"

21

"Yes, Sir." Bobby hopped on the truck bed to retrieve a tow chain from the tool box. He wrapped one end of it around their front bumper and connected the other to the tractor's hitch. The tractor was old, but Alcide kept it in top shape and it easily pulled the truck.

Bobby and Clyde rode in exasperated silence behind the tractor. They were so glad to be moving again the brothers hardly noticed the burned kerosene fumes filling their cab. Alcide stopped in front of the gas pump at Jesse's and Bobby unhitched the chain.

"Three gallons, please, Mr. LeBeau," Clyde said.

"Only three gallons? That won't take you far."

Clyde shrugged. "That's about all the money we got right now. We'll get work soon and then we can fill 'er up."

"You boys really need a new truck," Jesse said as he started pumping gas. "This thing is way past being on its last legs, and you still owe me for the last two times I fixed it."

"Yes, Sir, and we'll pay you just as soon as we get some work," Clyde said.

"Say, maybe y'all could work for the oil company that's gonna start drilling 'round here soon. They always need trucks."

"We're just waitin' 'til they start, so's we can offer them our services. We get steady work, we can buy a new truck," Bobby said.

"Biggest problem I see is I don't think they'll hire you with this old rattletrap. You're gonna need something more reliable."

Alcide motioned Clyde aside. They talked for a few moments, shook hands, then Alcide chugged away on his tractor.

Clyde paid for the gas and the brothers drove off down Levee Road. Two lanes of gravel, dirt, and potholes, it started at River Road, near the Mississippi River levee, then ran west until it disappeared five miles later into *Eau Noir* Swamp.

"Mr. Doucet wants us to pull some stumps for him tomorrow morning. That'll get us a little gas money, but Jesse's right," Clyde said. "We need a good truck to get that oil company to give us jobs. They ain't gonna trust this old thing to do nothin' for them. Only we can't even afford a tank of gas."

"We gotta get some big money and a new truck before all them truckin' jobs are gone."

Gravel crunched under their tires as Clyde drove on. Bobby stared straight ahead. "Where're we gonna get some money?" Clyde shouted out the window.

Clyde was five feet seven inches tall, medium build, with long, wavy brown hair parted in the middle and slicked back on both sides. He rarely smiled or laughed. Anyone who thought his quiet demeanor meant a lack of intelligence was unaware he finished near the top of his high school class. After graduation, he did odd jobs and scraped together enough money to buy the old truck he drove, but his dream of starting a trucking company with Bobby was all but gone. Twenty-five years old now, he still lived at home with his parents and brother.

Folks said Bobby reminded them of a big, friendly puppy.

"All he needs is a tail to wag," his aunt said.

23

Two years younger and four inches taller than his brother, Bobby's easygoing manner and quick laugh instantly won him friends. His high school classmates voted him most popular boy and most likely to succeed.

His teachers shook their heads when that last award was announced. "Class clown would be more appropriate," his math teacher muttered.

The brothers drove on in silence.

When they reached LeBlanc's Grocery Store, Clyde said, "Look what Mr. LeBlanc's done." He slowed down in front of the store. "He's let some bank from Baton Rouge use Maw Maw's old house to open up a branch way out here. Know what, Bobby? A bank's got lots of money inside. Wonder how we could get some of it? Let's go see what Mr. LeBlanc can tell us about the 'First Bank of Baton Rouge, Levee Branch,'" he said as he read the sign on the front of the building. "Let me do the talkin'. Maybe what you said earlier would work."

"Huh? What'd I say?"

"Never mind," Clyde said and opened the door to the store.

When Harve LeBlanc's mother-in-law could no longer live by herself in Plaquemine, he built a small frame house for her next to his store so his wife, Bea, could care for her mother. Known throughout the community as Maw Maw, she lived there beside the Mississippi River levee, in the shade of a gigantic oak tree, until she died two years ago.

"Morning, Mr. LeBlanc," Bobby said as the store's screen door slammed shut behind them.

"Shut up, I tole you," Clyde hissed through clenched teeth.

Harve's eyebrows drew together as he turned to look at the clock on the wall behind him. "Uh, afternoon, boys. What can I do for you?"

"Our momma wants a loaf of bread and some grits," Clyde said.

Bobby turned toward Clyde with a questioning look in his eye.

"Coming right up."

"They open up a bank in Maw Maw's old house?" Clyde asked.

"Yeah. Mr. Lyons, a banker man from Baton Rouge, said he wanted to open a branch here in Levee. They thought folks might want a safe place to put their money when that oil company starts drilling. We ain't used her house for nothin' but to store stuff in since she died, so I rented it to him. He changed a few things, put up his sign, moved in a big safe, and made a regular little bank there."

At mention of the word safe, Bobby looked at Clyde and grinned.

"Yeah, we heard about the drillin' that's coming and hope we can get some work from them," Clyde said.

"If you boys do, or get any money from towing or something, you might want to deposit it in the bank to keep it safe," Harve said.

"That's a good idea," Bobby said.

Clyde nudged his brother in the ribs and said, "I tole you . . ."

"Here's your bread and grits, and here's a little lagniappe for your momma." Harve added a small box of raisins to Clyde's purchase. "Anything else I can get you?"

"No, Sir. That'll be all, thank you," Clyde said. He dug in his jeans pocket and found just enough change left to pay for the groceries.

After the screen door slammed shut behind them, Bobby said, "Momma didn't say nothin' about no bread and grits."

"Of course not, you idiot, but we couldn't just go in and ask Mr. LeBlanc about the bank. He would of thought there's something funny about that."

"Oh, I get it. Just act natural while we check the place out. Smart thinkin', Clyde."

Clyde shook his head and slid into the driver's seat.

~

Bobby and Clyde arrived at Alcide Doucet's place early the next morning. The weathered Cajun farmer met them in his front yard.

"Good morning, boys," he said. "Glad you could make it. Like I told you yesterday Clyde, I been clearing an old pasture out behind the house and I got it all done except for getting rid of some tree stumps. Think you can pull them up for me? They're too much for my Fordson."

"Oh, yes, Sir," Bobby answered. "Just show us where they's at."

Bobby slid to the middle of the truck's bench seat and Alcide rode shotgun. He directed them down a path beside his house. Arriving at the field, he got out, opened a gate for them, got back in, pointed and said, "Across this field to that back corner." The truck bounced and rattled over old cotton rows as Clyde steered it across the field. Alcide got out again to open another gate.

"This here field. See all them stumps? I'd like you to pull 'em up and lay 'em to one side. I'll have my man come out tomorrow and pick 'em up and throw 'em on that trash pile," he said, pointing to an already high stack of tree limbs and brush. "Then I'll put some gas on it and burn it all up."

"Sure thing," Bobby said and jumped out. He walked to the nearest stump and guided Clyde as he backed the truck.

Clyde's truck, a gin pole truck, had two four-inch diameter pipes, each ten feet long, mounted to the rear corners of the truck bed. A large bolt passed through a pad eye at the lower end of each pole, so they could pivot up and down. The upper ends of the gin poles were fastened together by another bolt, so they looked like an inverted V. A heavy chain stretched from the poles to a frame made of pipes at the front of the truck's bed. Once very sturdy, the frame now was riddled with rust holes. The chains usually held the poles at a forty-five degree angle behind the truck, but they could be adjusted to lower the gin poles if the job called for it. A rusty steel cable with a hook at its working end passed through a large pulley dangling from the peak of the inverted V, then ran forward to a hydraulic-powered winch mounted just behind the truck's cab.

The gin poles were emblazoned with 'Barré Brothers TruckingCo.' Bobby had taken the truck to Robichaux's Sign Shop to have the name painted on them. Neither brother thought anything of the wording until Clyde's former high school English teacher told him it should read 'Trucking Co.' not 'Truck Co.' Clyde corrected it as best he could.

When the peak of the gin poles was over the stump, Bobby motioned for Clyde to stop. Bobby wrapped a stout chain around it while Clyde set the brakes of the truck and got out. He started the winch and paid out cable until Bobby grabbed the hook and attached it to the chain. Clyde engaged the winch. It groaned as the cable pulled tight and the truck lowered a little in the rear and the front raised a bit. The stump moved and quivered, then broke free in a shower of dirt. The truck bounced and pitched and settled back down. Clyde paid out the winch cable and Bobby guided the stump to the side of the hole. He unwrapped the chain and directed Clyde to the next one.

They continued working and pulled the last stump as the sun sank half-way below the horizon. They bounced back across the old cotton field to Doucet's house.

Alcide sat in a rocking chair on his front porch with a half empty bottle of Jax beer in his hand. "All finished, boys?"

"Yes Sir, Mr. Doucet," Bobby said. "Want us to take you back out there so you can see?"

"No, I seen enough of that field for one day." He handed Clyde an envelope. "Here's your money, but count it to be sure it's right."

Clyde looked in the envelope and flipped through the bills. "It's all here, Mr. Doucet. Thank you, Sir."

Bobby and Clyde got in the truck and started for home. "Let's stop at Mike's Place for a beer," Bobby said.

"No. We're going straight home now and tomorrow we're going to the bank and open us up an account."

"What for? We don't need no bank account."

"Maybe not, but we need a good excuse to get in that bank and look around real good. You forget about all the money in there?"

"Oh, yeah, and we're gonna make it ours, right Clyde?"

"We're sure gonna try to."

A faint orange glow was beginning to brighten the eastern sky when Bobby shook Clyde awake. "Get up," he said. "We gotta get to the bank."

"Go back to sleep," Clyde said. "Banks don't open this early."

"When, then?"

"About ten."

Bobby groaned and lay back down.

After Mrs. Barré fixed breakfast for her family, and her husband left for his job on the ferry in Port Allen, Clyde yawned, stretched, and said, "Me and Bobby're going to that new bank beside Mr. LeBlanc's store and open an account. Mr. Doucet paid us good money to pull some stumps for him yesterday and we want to keep it safe."

Bobby grinned at his brother.

"That's a good thing to do," their mother said.

Bobby and Clyde piled into the truck and drove to the bank.

"Just stay with me and don't say nothin'," Clyde said.

~

A pale, thin man looked up from behind a large oak desk when the Barré brothers entered the bank. Several piles of paper were neatly stacked on the desk. A large safe dominated the rest of the room, which had been Maw Maw's living room. The banker rose and stepped around the desk to greet his visitors. Slightly pudgy around the waist and wearing a gray suit with a conservative tie, he extended his hand to Clyde.

"Good morning, gentlemen. I'm Ray Lyons, manager of the Levee Branch of the First Bank of Baton Rouge. What can I do for you?"

Bobby looked around the room. Clyde grabbed his arm and pulled him along.

"We want to open a bank account," Clyde said.

"A joint account or one for each of you?"

Bobby looked at his brother. "An account for our business," Clyde said.

"Oh, and what is that business?"

"Barré Brothers Trucking Company."

"All right, Mr. Barré, have a seat." Lyons pushed several pieces of paper toward Clyde and handed him a fountain pen. "Just fill the blanks in these forms. Do you want both of you to be able to sign checks?"

"No, just me," Clyde said.

Bobby looked at Clyde with a question in his eye, but then he shrugged and got up. His chair scraped across the floor and tumbled over with a crash. He righted it and walked toward the safe.

"Come back here, Bobby," Clyde said, but Bobby ignored him.

"It's all right, Mr. Barré. Just finish filling out the paperwork, and we can get your account set up."

Bobby ran his hands across the top of the safe and felt around the door. He leaned over and looked at the combination lock on the front. He twirled the dial and listened to it click as it spun. "Sure looks strong," Bobby said.

"It is," Lyons said. "Your money will be safe here."

Clyde finished filling out the forms and handed them to Lyons.

"Everything looks good, Mr. Barré. All I need is a deposit of at least five dollars to open your account."

"We got more'n that," Bobby said and grinned.

Clyde frowned at Bobby, but handed Alcide Doucet's envelope to the banker. Lyons counted the money, made out a deposit slip, signed it, and handed it to Clyde.

"We're all done, Mr. Barré. I'll put your money in the safe and you can be on your way." He walked to the safe and hunched over it as he turned the dial. It whirred and clicked as he spun it first to the right, then to the left and back right again.

Bobby stood behind Lyons and craned his neck trying to see where the banker stopped the dial. He bobbed his head left, right, up, and down but could not see over Lyons' shoulders.

31

Lyons finished and dropped his hands. Bobby whirled around to face the opposite wall.

"Thanks, Mr. Lyons," Clyde said. "Our money's safe, so we'll be going now." They started toward the door, but Clyde stopped and turned around. "You live here, Mr. Lyons?"

"Only during the week. I go back to Baton Rouge on Friday afternoons to spend the weekend with my family. Why?"

"Just wonderin'. Seems like a nice little house, uh, bank. Thanks again."

He turned and walked out with Bobby.

"That didn't do no good," Bobby said. "I couldn't see none of the places he stopped. How we gonna open that safe if we don't know the combination?"

"We ain't gonna open it, we're gonna take it."

"What?" Bobby said.

"Don't you see? That safe's just sittin' there on Maw Maw's living room floor, so all we gotta do is grab it with the cable on the truck and drag it out and take it someplace where we can open it and get all the money. Simple."

"Yeah, but how we gonna hook up to it and get it outta there without nobody seein' us?"

"I ain't figgered that out yet."

~

Two weeks later, on a Wednesday afternoon, Bobby and Clyde stopped for gas at LeBeau's filling station.

"Y'all going to the *fais do do* Saturday night?" Jesse asked.

"Ain't heard nothin' about it," Bobby said. "Where it's at?"

"The high school. Go read the flyer in my window. Should be some pretty girls there," Jesse said with a smirk.

The brothers went over to Jesse's window and Bobby read the flyer aloud. "*Fais do do* Saturday night. 8:00 'til midnight. New Roads HS gym. Johnny Arceneaux's band. Sounds like fun. Let's go, Clyde."

"I got it!" Clyde said. "This is it!"

"This is what?"

"Get in the truck."

Clyde paid for the gas and jumped behind the steering wheel. He burned rubber leaving.

"We ain't going to the dance Saturday night. We're going to the bank," Clyde said, as they drove toward home.

"What?"

"Think about it, Bobby. Everybody in town and half the parish will be at the dance. Mr. and Miz LeBlanc always go to every dance, and Mr. Lyons will be in Baton Rouge. This is our chance to take the safe."

"Good thinkin', Clyde, but how we gonna do it?"

"I haven't thought out all the details yet."

Clyde rubbed his chin as he continued down Levee Road.

Several minutes later Bobby said, "What you thinkin', Clyde?"

"We'll lower the gin poles until they're just as high as the bank's front window. Then I'll back the truck up and punch the poles right through the wall. You go through the hole and wrap the chain around the safe and hook it to the cable. Then you get back in and we drag it right out the hole in the wall. We'll take it way back in the woods behind the house and cover it with tree limbs and stuff until we figure out how to open it. Ma and Pa won't be around that time of night. Easy as pie."

~

Saturday afternoon found the Barré brothers working on their truck. They replaced the chains holding up the gin poles with longer ones. Clyde started the winch and lowered the poles until the point of the V reached head height.

"That should clear the porch and go right through the wall. Tie a white rag on the poles, so people can see them in the dark," he said.

Bobby did, then put their longest tow chain in the tool box. The brothers were so excited they could hardly eat supper that night.

"Y'all going to the *fais do do* tonight?" Mr. Barré asked.

Bobby gulped and choked on a piece of fried catfish. "No. Yes. Maybe," he said.

"Are you, or aren't you?"

"We haven't decided," Clyde said. "We'll probably drive by and see who's there and decide then." They helped their mother clear the table and left the kitchen.

34

"Bye, Ma. Bye, Pa."

The hall clock struck half past eight as they walked out the front door.

"We got everything?" Bobby asked.

"I think so."

Clyde drove by the gym to be sure the dance was still on. Pickups, cars, and horse drawn buggies filled the parking lot. The sounds of a guitar, two wailing fiddles, an accordion, and Johnny Arceneaux singing "Allons à Lafayette" reached their ears. A rousing Cajun Saturday night *fais do do* was in full swing.

"Good. Let's go see if the LeBlancs are home," Clyde said.

They drove by the store and everything was dark except for a dim night light Harve always left on. The bank was also dark. Clyde drove past LeBlanc's, made a u-turn, came back, turned in the driveway, and stopped in front of the bank. He backed up until the gin poles were at the edge of the front porch. He stopped the truck and the brothers got out.

Bobby took the chain out of the toolbox and laid it on the porch, so it would be ready when the front wall went down.

"Let's go," he said and rubbed his hands together.

Clyde got behind the wheel and put the truck in reverse. He eased out on the clutch and the truck inched backward. The gin poles crossed over the porch and punched through the front window of the bank. Glass shattered and spewed in all directions. The truck continued its slow retreat and the bank's front wall splintered as the gin poles pushed the wooden planks aside.

Bobby leaped onto the porch and peered through the hole. As soon as the peak of the poles was over the safe he yelled, "Stop." Then he climbed through the wall, dragging the tow chain behind him. *Just like a ghost, chain and all,* he smiled to himself.

Clyde put the transmission in neutral and set the parking brake, but left the engine idling. He got out of the cab and started the winch engine. Bobby already had a gloved hand on the cable hook, so Clyde paid out some slack.

"That's enough," Bobby called.

Clyde jumped on the porch and climbed through the wall. Bobby had begun to wrap the chain around the safe. Clyde helped him – up one side, over the top, down the other side, under the safe, around it, and back to the top. They looped both ends of the chain through the hook on the winch cable.

"I'll take up the slack and you stop me if it ain't right," Clyde said. "When we get it outside we'll haul it up close, chain it to the truck, so it don't swing back and forth and head for the woods." He crawled through the wall and went to his winch controls. He engaged the clutch and slowly took up the slack in the cable. The winch groaned and the truck shook.

"That's good," Bobby called. "I'm coming out."

Bobby crawled through the wall, jumped off the porch and stood to one side, out of the way.

Clyde released the parking brake and put the truck in gear. He let out the clutch and the truck inched forward a foot and stalled. He restarted the engine and tried again, but got no farther.

"C'mon, Clyde. We need to get out of here."

"I'm tryin' but seems like we're anchored to the ground."

"Hit it hard."

Clyde gave the old truck more gas and let the clutch out again. It lurched forward and the front wheels left the ground. He gave it more gas and the front end reared up so far he feared it would topple over backward. He let off the gas and pushed in the clutch. The truck slammed down with a deafening crash as all the tools in the box clanged together. Badly shaken, Clyde got out to see if the truck was damaged. The engine was still running and the truck looked to be in no more pieces than when they started.

"Did it move?" He asked Bobby.

"The truck did, but I don't think the safe budged."

"Go check it."

Bobby jumped back onto the porch and peered through the hole in the wall. "It ain't moved an inch," he said.

"That don't make no sense," Clyde said. "That safe can't be too heavy for us to drag it across the floor. I'll try again."

Bobby walked around to the passenger's side of the truck. Clyde revved the engine and eased the clutch out. The front end began to rise again.

He let off on the gas and let the truck bang down, then he revved it again. The front end raised higher than it had before.

Headlights swept across the ground in front of them and momentarily blinded Clyde. The truck crashed back to earth.

"Somebody's coming," Bobby yelled. He opened the passenger's door and jumped in the cab. "We gotta go, Clyde."

Clyde put the truck in gear once more and floored it. The front end rose as before, but not as far. The Barré brothers, looking out the windshield at the night sky, were slung violently left, then right as a tearing, ripping crash split the night. The engine revved and the rear wheels dug in. The old truck leaped forward and the front wheels hit the ground.

"We did it!" Bobby shouted. "We got it out!"

A car stopped in the store parking lot. A man and a woman jumped out and stood silhouetted in its headlights. Clyde gunned the truck across the meadow in front of LeBlanc's store. With the headlights off, he hoped they would not be able to identify his truck as he raced toward the road. They bounced through a shallow ditch beside the road and heard the reassuring sound of gravel crunching under their tires.

"We made it,' Bobby said. "They couldn't of seen who we was in the dark."

"I'll turn on Landry Road, and we can tie down the safe so it don't swing too much," Clyde said.

He turned onto the road and stopped.

Bobby hopped out and ran around to the back of the truck. "Clyde! Come see what happened! You ain't gonna believe this."

~

"What was that?" Bea LeBlanc asked Harve.

38

"A truck racing away from the bank with its lights off."

"At this time of night?"

"Let's go see."

As they approached the bank, Bea said, "Look. There's a big hole in the front wall. They ruined Maw Maw's house!"

"What the...?" Harve said. He climbed onto the front porch. "I think somebody tried to rob the bank!"

"Did you see who it was? Did they get anything?" Bea asked.

"I dunno. There's chains wrapped around the safe but it's still here. Doesn't look like anything's missing except Maw Maw's front wall. Hey, there's a cable across the porch --"

"What's this?" Bea said. She touched her toe to something lying on the ground. Harve jumped off the porch to see what she had found.

"Some pipes. No, wait. They're gin poles off a truck. And there's the winch. That must have been the loud noise we heard ... when it ripped off."

Harve looked at the poles more closely. "I guess we know who did this, Bea."

There in the faint moonlight were two gin poles with B a r r é Brothers TruckingCo. emblazoned on them.

"The gin poles are still hooked to the safe," Harve said. "They must have been trying to drag it out of the bank but tore their poles and winch off instead. I guess they didn't know Mr. Lyons had that big block of concrete poured under the house before he brought his safe in and how he had it

39

welded to steel rods in that concrete." Harve slapped his knew with his hat and chuckled.

Bea just shook her head. "Bonnie and Clyde, they ain't."

The Apartment

by

Ramon Del Villar

The Apartment
by Ramon del Villar

Alberto Treviño sat in the comfort of the first class cabin of the Avianca direct flight from Houston, Texas, to Bogota, Colombia. As he finished his after-dinner brandy, Alberto reflected on how easily he had become accustomed to this lifestyle.

As one of the top-level acquisition attorneys in a large Houston oil corporation, he regularly traveled to Latin America. His native fluency in Spanish and his warm personality made him ideal for these kinds of deals.

Unlike the icy-professionalism needed in the states, working with Latin American businesses required establishing rapport with the local attorneys and being able to communicate with them in flawless Spanish.

The PA buzzed to life announcing the arrival to Bogota and Alberto went over his travel documents to check that everything was in order.

Once in the airport terminal, after clearing immigration and customs, Alberto walked to the transportation hub. As expected, a limousine waited there to drive him over to the twenty-story building where his employer owned an extremely well-appointed apartment on the twelfth floor.

The apartment was a necessity in the still charged and dangerous atmosphere of the Colombian capital, where kidnappings and muggings were a brutal reality. This particular building had been chosen by the corporate planners because, besides being in one of the best districts of the capital, it was guarded by professionals with the most up-to-date security technology. But it was the dogs that made the biggest difference.

Every floor was patrolled by pairs of Dobermans trained to trace and detect intruders. In the sophisticated capital, this unique feature earned it the nickname "The Doberman Building."

Corporate was well aware of the fact that apartment buildings in Bogota were frequently the victims of thieves, who could sack an apartment of all its valuables in a matter of seconds. It was rumored the robbers called themselves *apartamenteros,* an amorphous description commonly defined as apartment builders, apartment owners, or apartment service-providers, but which those in the know understood as apartment burglars.

The car approached the shiny blue high-rise. The driver got out, fetched the luggage from the trunk, and opened the door for Alberto.

"At 9:30 PM then, Mr. Treviño?" The chauffeur inquired in Spanish.

"Yes, Paco. And I'm planning to go do some girl-watching tonight after dinner," Alberto responded back in Spanish.

"There is a new place that just opened up, if you care to try it?"

"Excellent. I'll see you tonight." Alberto turned and headed in through the automatic revolving doors.

Of course, Alberto was a happily married man and was not about to cheat on his wife. But, during his frequent trips to Bogota, he enjoyed going to some of the elegant discos in the city, tossing back a couple of drinks, and enjoying a flirtatious conversation with some girls. Never more than that.

"Your identification, sir," the young security guard prompted.

"Here you go," Alberto handed over his passport.

It was a little aggravating, going through the routine of properly identifying himself to the security detail at the lobby, given that he was a constant guest here. Still, they were only doing their job. Soon, Alberto made his way to the elegant apartment, one of the four exclusive apartments on the twelfth floor.

After unpacking his bags, he walked over to the study with its large windows overlooking the beautiful city. The metropolis had been built on the sides of towering mountains, affording almost all of the high rises a marvelous view.

Alberto took in the splendor for a moment before picking up the inter-phone. He ordered a carafe of fresh coffee from the cafeteria on the second floor. Colombian coffee is among the very best in the world and this exclusive building had carafes available 24/7, a perk for its affluent residents.

When the coffee service arrived, Alberto was already hard at work at his laptop contacting the Colombian attorneys he needed to meet with and outlining the topics he would address with them.

Taking a break, Alberto poured himself a cup and took out a box of 956 Puerto Rican Short Panatella cigars, his favorite brand and size. Returning to the view, he enjoyed a few puffs, before going back to his work.

He continued setting-up appointments and exchanging memos and comments over email as well as over the phone until his cell alarm rang indicating that it was 8:00 PM. It was already dark outside, but Alberto had been too immersed in his work to notice the sunset and was a little disappointed because, in spite of his profession, Alberto was a poet at heart and greatly enjoyed nature's majesty.

Alberto secured the documents and his laptop in his Hartmann briefcase and headed to the en-suite bathroom. Turning on the water, he prepared his Schick Titanium razor to shave inside the shower.

Sometime later, he was combing his hair and dressing in a navy blue suit with a lime-green tie that made a stark combination but looked great.

Alberto knew, from his years of traveling throughout Latin America, it would never be proper to go out for dinner in leisure clothes. A tie and a jacket are *de rigeur* for a night in the city.

At exactly 9:30, his cell phone rang. It was Paco, who was waiting with the limo. Alberto wasted no time and soon they were on their way to "Los Camaradas."

"It's a nice mom-and-pop place, but elegant. The food is real authentic Colombian." Paco peaked in the rearview mirror at his passenger. "I think you will enjoy it, Mr. Trevino."

"You have always been spot on with your recommendations, Paco," Alberto said with a wry smile. "I'm sure this one will be just as deliciously enjoyable."

Alberto climbed back into the limo several hours later, satiated with the home-cooking of the restaurant. He would need to remember to give Paco an extra hefty tip.

"Paco, surprise me. I want to go girl-watching as I said, so take me to a fashionable disco."

"Yes, sir," responded Paco. "They just opened a new one that I'm sure will contain the prettiest girls in Bogota tonight."

"What are we waiting for?" said Alberto with a big smile.

They got to the disco and Alberto discovered Paco was a true expert on the subject of dining and entertainment. The place was elegantly appointed and already half full of beautiful girls and young men who all seemed to be under thirty. Couples gyrated wildly on the dance floor to the newest pop music.

After a couple of hours, Alberto realized the gentleman seated at a table just across the dance floor from his own had been watching him for some time. He looked to be in his forties also. Alberto, at forty-two, was aware most of the people in attendance were under thirty, which made him feel a bit of empathy for the other guy at first. They exchanged glances and Alberto smiled and nodded politely.

A pair of long curvy legs distracted him from the stranger. The legs were attached to a lusciously endowed young lady, who walked by his table and graced him with a flirty smile. Alberto smiled back, but made sure his expression showed he was not interested in a one-night stand. Shrugging, golden ringlets bouncing as she turned her head, the beauty joined a group of friends near the dance floor.

Looking up, Alberto was startled to find that the stranger was now standing in front of his table.

"Hi, I could not help but notice that we are about the only two guys who are not accompanied by beautiful girls here and I thought that maybe we could sit together. Don't take it wrong. I'm not gay, just thought that it would be nice to have someone to exchange impressions with." The stranger extended a hand in friendship.

Alberto, who had been a marine lieutenant in Iraq during the First Gulf War and sometimes missed the camaraderie of fellow soldiers, didn't hesitate. He stood up, extended his hand, and gestured for the man to join him at his table.

"I'm Alberto."

"Nice to meet you. I'm Luis," his guest introduced himself. "Your Spanish is very good, for an American."

"How did you know I'm an American?" Alberto inquired, taken aback by Luis's perceptiveness.

"I was a captain in the Colombian army and did a lot of missions. You become very good at spotting little things that can be valuable intel."

"I too served. In the marines…"

"Semper Fi, friend," Luis lifted his glass and they toasted.

Several hours passed as the two former soldiers exchanged stories from their respective military experiences.

After ordering another round of drinks, Alberto asked his new friend, "So, Luis, what do you do for a living?"

"I'm an investor."

"What kind of investments?"

"Apartment buildings, mainly. And you Alberto, what do you do?"

"I'm an attorney, working for an oil company in Houston, Texas."

"Yes, it is obvious you are not hurting for money," commented Luis, pointing at Alberto's gold Piaget watch.

"Well, friend, you don't seem to be in bad shape, either," Alberto replied, pointing to his friend's gold Rolex President.

They watched a new group of beautiful ladies dancing, commenting on their features. Of course, they joked about the couples that made out in the more secluded booths.

"You know, Alberto, I have not been completely honest with you."

"What do you mean," responded Alberto thinking to himself that maybe Luis was gay after all and trying to score with him.

"Well, I am not really an investor."

"You're not?" Alberto was kind of surprised by the comment. "What are you then?"

"I am an *apartamentero*."

"You build apartments?"

"No, I burglarize apartment buildings."

For a moment Alberto thought that his new friend was pulling his leg, but the serious look on Luis's countenance showed he was telling the truth.

"Well, you must be very good at that because you're obviously well-off."

"Yes, I am, but don't worry, I wouldn't even dream of burglarizing your apartment."

Alberto did not really know what to answer, so he blurted out, "Well, I am not afraid. The building I stay in while in Bogota is supposed to be impossible to rob. It's the Doberman Building."

Luis smiled, "I know the place. You are right. It's *almost* impregnable."

There was a semi-ironic tone in his voice, but then he added more lightheartedly, "Let's forget about our occupations and continue enjoying the view. That redhead over there has some plump hips, don't you think?"

They both laughed good-naturedly. It was almost 4 AM when the crowds began to thin. Alberto began feeling the tiredness of travel.

"What do you say we call it a night?" he suggested.

"Agreed. It's getting late."

Once outside, Alberto offered Luis a ride unsure if he had transportation. Luis pointed to his brand new black Mercedes S550. When the limo approached, they shook hands.

"Well, my friend, it was a pleasure meeting you."

"Likewise," Luis replied. "Here, take my card."

"Thank you," Alberto took the offered card and produced his own. "Here, this is mine. Okay, Luis, see you soon. Be sure not to get into my apartment."

Luis smiled, "I wouldn't do that, not to a fellow comrade at arms."

~

The days became extremely busy for Alberto. Though he thought a couple times of calling Luis and having a drink with his new friend, his business negotiations went well into the night.

Before he knew it was the eve of his return to Houston. It was late, but, before going to bed that night, he decided to call the phone number listed on Luis's card. The phone rang, until Luis's voicemail picked-up. Alberto left a short message saying he had to leave Bogota the next day and would try to contact Luis the next time he visited the city.

Heading straight to bed, Alberto was sound asleep the moment his head hit the pillow.

~

The barking of dogs awakened Alberto. Groggy from sleep, he thought that it was strange that the dogs barked. The Dobermans were specially trained and never barked. He was about to rise from his bed and check it out when the barking stopped. Part of his mind told him something was wrong, but then he reassured himself, this was the most secure building in the city after all. Alberto allowed himself to descend once more into the sweet darkness of sleep.

~

Promptly at 6 AM, Alberto's cell phone alarm rang. Silencing it, he flung his legs over the side of the bed and reached for his watch. He found it on the nightstand, just as he had left it in the evening. Then Alberto gave a startled cry. Under the Piaget there was what seemed to be a business card.

He picked up the card and noted it was Luis's, only it had a message scrawled on the back in messy handwriting.

It read: "Alberto, I just came by to say goodbye and perhaps share a nightcap, but you were sound asleep and I didn't want to bother you. Have a nice trip and I will see you next time you are around."

Frantically, Alberto got up and went through all his belongings; his papers, his laptop, everything was there; nothing had been taken.

Sinking back onto the edge of the bed, Alberto threw his head back and enjoyed a good laugh.

The Pit

by

Meg Hafdahl

The Pit
by Meg Hafdahl

The first time I committed murder I was six years old. I knew it was wrong. But my Uncle Jeremy smelled of moldy leather and dusty cigarettes.

He watched us on Wednesday nights, when Mom had her night class at the technical college. That last night he brought us a pizza. It had green peppers on it. He snickered when he told me to pick them out of the hot cheese.

"Ah Missy," he said when I burned my tiny fingers. "You clumsy nut."

I knew I was going to bring him to The Pit. It was the end of summer and soon it would be impossible to get him there. Here in Minnesota, summer changes into fall over one night. There is simply no more warmth and the leaves instantly turn orange. I figured I had only a few decent summer days left. Jeremy put baby Dawson to bed with a bottle he warmed in the microwave. I had to help him with the buttons; he would have melted the plastic if I hadn't helped. He was drunk, of course. There was never a time he wasn't listing to the side and hiccupping like a cartoon character with a jug marked XXX in its paws.

Then I said, "We should go The Pit."

He bent his greasy head back and laughed.

"It's still hot out." I crossed my arms and tightened my brows, so I looked like I was going to cry. Jeremy hated when I cried. He would usually leave me alone with a handful of toilet paper and take a smoke break out on the front porch until I stopped. "And school's coming and it's gonna get cold, this is my last chance."

I watched as he wiped his red nose with the back of his hand. He considered my face, strained and quivering as though I was on the precipice of a tantrum.

"Twenty minutes," he grumbled.

I rushed into the bathroom and climbed up onto the toilet to reach my swimsuit hanging on the shower rod. It was still damp from when Dawson and I had gone to The Pit that afternoon. I took off my nightgown, the one with the ponies jumping over a fluorescent rainbow on the front, and left it in a pile with my undies. I looked in the mirror as I raked my brown hair back into a bun. I knew it was murder, because I was looking into my own eyes and not stopping. As I stood in the cramped bathroom of our tiny bungalow on River Street, I knew precisely what I was doing.

We left sleeping Dawson and hiked up the steep hill to The Pit. My flip flops crunched beneath me in the night. Uncle Jeremy carried a plastic shopping bag with my towel inside. The orange glow at the end of the cigarette tucked between his lips was the only light. My eyes grew accustomed to the darkness as we made our way through the wooded gravel path.

Then we arrived. The moon was visible now, and its grey light reflected on the water like a dream. We now had to make our way down the rocky incline to swim.

"We nee' ta be back by ten or your mommy's gonna kill me," Jeremy slurred as he slid down the embankment on his ass. The cigarette didn't fall from his mouth.

56

I knew he wouldn't get in the water right away. But I had a plan. I slipped my flip flops off and put a cautious toe into the water. I took in the small stretch of shore; there were no teenagers skinny-dipping or night strollers walking their dogs.

We were alone.

I got in the black water slowly as he watched from the rocks. I waded out to the middle of The Pit. It was very deep, endlessly deep.

The Pit was named for its past as a mining pit, iron ore, before it was stripped bare and flooded. Some of us locals swim in The Pit. We like to avoid the tourist lakes with the rental boats and the overpriced pop.

I got all the way up to my neck before I felt it. The thing in the pit, my thing, caressed my bare legs with its familiar, ghostly fingers. Then it pressed firmer, pleased to see me, and I could feel the tentacles, vaguely sticky and strong around my stomach. It would not hurt me. I knew this from the first time it had tugged at my toes when I was barely four.

It had chosen me when I still had puffy swim diapers under my pink suit. I was scared of the sensation of something underneath the surface touching me at first; I had watched most of *Jaws* on cable with my older cousins. But then there was a warm buzz in my little head; a string of comforting words as it squeezed around me. It understood me. It liked to hear my dark thoughts, the real ugly, bloody ideas that Mom would usually slap me for. She said I couldn't say things like that out loud. My thoughts scared her. But I didn't need to even say them from my mouth to The Pit. Instead my thing would make me feel special for having my thoughts.

It loved me.

With a sideways look to make sure Uncle Jeremy was watching, I pretended to struggle. I dipped my head under the surface and pin wheeled my arms as though I couldn't swim. As I bobbed back up, I shouted and writhed rather dramatically. The thing, my thing, unfurled its gentle hold on me; it knew what was happening too.

I could see Uncle Jeremy getting up on his unsteady feet, his stub of a cigarette finally forgotten, falling from his mouth in a fiery streak. He didn't bother to remove his beloved motorcycle boots before he ran into the water.

It was nice he cared.

I had the quickest flash of something like regret. This was my last chance to stop. I didn't have to act out my thoughts.

But I wanted to.

"Melissa!" he screamed, as he doggy paddled toward me. I kept thrashing and coughing and I called his name in return. "I got you, I got you." He tried to grab my shoulder and that's when I stopped struggling and pushed away.

I could never drown in The Pit. The Pit would never let me. The thing inside the water was my buoy keeping me afloat and safe.

Uncle Jeremy waded next to me, his lips began to tighten up and his dark eyes looked stormy. "Is this a joke Missy? Is this a fucking joke?"

He almost seemed sober.

I smiled.

Then he felt The Pit too. It must have grabbed him around his ankle because he jerked suddenly and his head was under the water before I could blink. Then he came back up, coughing and snorting for real. I stayed where I was, watching him go drown while I lazily kicked my legs to stay upright. I knew The Pit would do what I wanted. It had told me so. It had told me without really talking.

He tried to scream, but there was too much water in his mouth and coming out of his nostrils. He clawed up at the water. Just his hands were above the surface, angry, scratching claws. And then my Uncle Jeremy was gone, pulled underneath. I waited to make sure he didn't come up like a floating cork.

When I got home, I put my nightgown on, the same one with the ponies, and wrung out my swimsuit. I put it back on the shower rod and watched TV and ate cold pizza with the peppers pulled off until Mom pushed through the front door and asked where Uncle Jeremy had run off to.

I told her that he said something about meeting a girl on Fox Bluff. She got red and huffed that she would kill him; she would just kill him for leaving me and Dawson alone. I smiled at her.

I had already taken care of it.

~

Seven summers later, Aiden Todd went straight down like an anchor.

It had been a hot day and his pale, freckled skin had called to me from the shore. I had been at The Pit alone until Aiden showed up. I spent most every day there. Even when The Pit was bursting with squealing kids and horny teenagers, I could find a place to float and be with my Pit. But I preferred to

59

come when it was silent and the water was still. I could share my scattered thoughts, a steady stream of dark ideas.

The Pit listened.

But then Aiden, a notorious bully, eased into the water with a pair of goggles swinging from his thick neck. I knew he had pushed my baby brother Dawson into the side of a vending machine on the last day of school. Dawson said Aiden laughed so hard tears dripped down his white cheeks. Now, as he swam towards me, Aiden leered at my burgeoning breasts and made disgusting comments. My Pit thing knew what to do; it clamped onto the bully's chubby legs. He went down, quick and silent.

I had the oddest sensation of jealousy. He was down there with The Pit, in its lair, and I couldn't be.

~

Six uneventful years went by. I was nineteen when Jake Tuttle asked me to murder again. He didn't know The Pit and I had done it before. We were in my bed, my zebra print sheets all pushed to the end of the mattress. Jake was naked, but I had slipped my panties back up.

"They're going to pin it on me. I'm going to be their prime suspect." He worked a toothpick into his mouth, considering his options. "I've got to have an alibi, Missy, something real solid, like lots of people to say I was there and I couldn't have done it."

"I'll do it," I shrugged.

Jake didn't hear me. "She's a real bitch, Missy. She hates me, screams at me, but she wants to get pregnant and trap me." He felt it necessary to invoke my rage apparently.

"I'll do it tomorrow." I handed him his boxers. "We'll make sure you have an alibi. But you have to get her to The Pit first. Tell her you'll meet her there late, um, let's say midnight. Don't text her about it though. The police will look at your texts."

Jake sat up, his scruffy face a mixture of relief and awe. "How? How will you do it at The Pit?"

I shook my head. "You just get her there and I'll take care of it."

"Are you going to stab her with something?" His words trailed off into a trembling whisper.

"She'll be gone." I kissed Jake on his bare shoulder.

"But Missy," he blinked, "if you're going to weigh her down into the water, like with something heavy, you're going to need me. You're too small." He pulled me into his chest and hugged me roughly to emphasize his point.

"No, no, you go to Dexter's."

"Miss..."

"Jake, I mean it. Just go to Dexter's right after dinner, around eight, and get real loud and invite the boys. Then go home with one of them, sleep on a couch. Oh and you should even flirt with that waitress, you know the one with all the moles on her face."

We laughed.

But then I pulled back and watched him. He stared past me, past the window. The toothpick hung from the corner of his mouth, limp, and forgotten.

He didn't think I could do it. I felt angry he didn't trust me, but mostly I was excited to prove him wrong.

He kissed me on the forehead before he rolled off the bed and retrieved his work jeans from a puddle of clothes on the floor. I loved Jake. I wanted him for myself although he was married and he drank too much and he smelled of stale cigarettes just as Uncle Jeremy had.

~

She came down the steep incline very slowly, testing each step with a tentative wiggle. Andrea Tuttle was still in her Taco Bell uniform, black greasy slacks and a white collared shirt. She even had the visor, with the recognizable bell stitched in yellow, on top of her blonde stringy hair. It was dark and so she couldn't see me wading up to my chin in the deep water. I could feel The Pit stroking my sides, reassuring me. It would help me. It wanted what I wanted.

I was surprised when she started to undress. Andrea shivered as she removed her uniform and left it on the narrow strip of sand. She placed her Taco Bell visor gingerly on top of her pile of clothes, as though it were a treasured keepsake. Jake's wife wore a bikini, the kind with string sides that embedded into her fleshy thighs and two tiny triangles that covered a small portion of her swinging breasts.

I thought of her picking the tight bottoms out of her ass crack as she wrapped hard shells in paper and scooped guacamole.

Andrea made her way into The Pit as slowly as she had crept down the hill. Honestly, I thought I was going to have to push her in, or pretend to drown again, or tell her some story about needing her help finding my pearl earring. But I had underestimated her want of Jake, her willingness to trust him.

"Jake?" She was up to her waist, her breasts skimming the water. "Jake you moron," she panted. "You better not scare me. Where the hell are you?" Her eyes were suspicious slits. I stayed still. The Pit swirled around me. It was nudging my legs like an anxious dog ready for the hunt.

Andrea pushed out a little deeper in to the black water, probably to avoid the chilly wind from hitting her naked back.

"Hi, Andrea!" I bobbed up and gave a dramatic wave.

She startled, twisting her head in every direction to see where my voice came from. I think she saw me, or at least made out my figure, because she began to dog paddle toward me. She thought I was her friend I suppose.

It happened so quickly, even faster than Aiden Todd. She was doing her little doggy kick and then she stopped. Her mouth gaped like a fish on a hook, surprised and angry. Andrea made a little soft sound, the whiny grumble of an indignant child refusing to believe life is indeed not fair. Then she was pulled backward with such force her hair whipped the water and her hands dug into the surface as though she were on a high ledge and she was scrambling for purchase. But of course, there was nothing to grab on to and so she sank down. Her hands and feet were in the air like an upturned beetle as her body was drawn into the blackness.

I backstroked in the new silence. After a while I felt The Pit come back to me; the pressure of its arms, its ghostly tentacles, its ephemeral body felt good against mine. I was half asleep, dozing in its embrace when I heard Jake on the shore. I knew he couldn't really be there; he was safe at Dexter's, so I figured it was a dream. I snuggled in closer to the water, ready to imagine it was Jake's arms around me, lifting me up. I wanted to pretend it was Jake's fingers lightly caressing my thighs.

"Psssssst. Psssst Melissa?" Jake's distinct gravelly voice whispered from the side of The Pit. "Missy?"

I felt nothing around me, no warmth or embrace. I could only hear Jake's voice, cutting and decidedly real, in the night.

Jake you moron.

He jumped in before I could protest. He should be far away, in popular and brightly lit Dexter's bar, playing pool with friends and telling bad jokes.

"Missy, is it done?" He was by my side in a few single strokes.

"Jesus, shut up." I pushed him. "Someone could walk by."

Jake nodded thoughtfully and put his muscular arms around me. "I'm sorry, is everything okay?"

I couldn't help grinning. "Yeah, everything is good."

We kissed then. He ran his hands all over me and I felt like I made him happy. I was useful. I tucked my head under his chin and I was going to chide him, gently, for not staying put, for leaving his golden alibi. But then his whole body quivered beside me.

I pushed back from him, to watch his expression. Jake's eyebrows were knit together in confusion. He was still floating in the water, but his arms cycled frantically.

No, no, no.

"Jake, c'mon, let's get out, let's get out." My voice was shaky. I stretched out my hands and tried to grab his wrists. He was dunked then, pulled quickly, and then released.

"Mi…." Jake garbled my name, his mouth filling with water.

"NO!" I slapped the water with both hands. "NO! NOT HIM!" I swam closer to Jake. The Pit was wrong. It had it all wrong.

I tried to pull him, but he was so big. And The Pit was wrapped around his ankle, or perhaps it had both legs by now. Jake went under again, his entire body trying to kick away to no avail. I could touch him still. I had my hands on his chest, and then he slipped further, I was holding his shoulders, then I pawed at his neck, and, finally, I held his fingers. I pulled wildly, feeling myself go with him, sensing the water up my nose and in my eyes. For a single second, I thought I would go with him, hang on to tightening grip and be in The Pit.

I let go. I had to.

I shuddered, the realization turning over in my stomach and my mind.

"nnnnoooNONONONO YOU STUPID FUCKING PIT!" I screeched at the night, at the now hushed water.

I could only hear my breath, ragged and desperate, as I tried to look down, tried to see the thing that had taken Jake. I had never seen it as a formed thing. Since I was a toddler, I had sensed its closeness, its affinity for me, but I had never seen it. I had only felt it on my skin and heard it in my head. But I knew The Pit, and I knew it was jealous.

65

It was jealous I loved Jake. Knowing this somehow made me angrier. Fire rushed through my veins, it was a complete and overwhelming anger I had never known.

"I hate you, I hate you, I hate you," I cried into the water. I wanted to kill it. I wanted to strangle it and make it stop being.

It touched me then, swished by my ankles with a tender graze. I kicked at it and spat in the water. I could only whimper and shake. The cold night was overtaking me, making my teeth chatter.

I was alone. My thing had paddled away into the deep, leaving me to bob in the black water like an unanchored raft. It was with them. It was with them and not me. Shivering and tired, I swam back toward the shore. For one hopeful instant, when my toes touched the first particles of sand, I thought it was The Pit reaching out for me. No. I was more alone than I felt was even possible. And it wasn't Jake whom I missed. I knew this fully. The Pit had abandoned me. My anger cooled and I could feel only an overwhelming loneliness.

"I'm sorry." My throat was raw from screaming.

I wanted to say more, I wanted to reason with The Pit, make it understand it had made a mistake, but it was alright, I forgave it, I loved it. But I was in the shallow end, my butt in the sand, and it probably couldn't hear my words or my mind.

I cried. I didn't want to go back. I couldn't walk up to my apartment, dripping Pit water, and go to sleep. I couldn't work another shift, or play video games with my baby brother Dawson, or swim on a hot summer day ever again. There had to be a conclusion. I couldn't walk away from The Pit.

As though it heard my thoughts, it appeared. Perhaps it had heard me all along, where ever I was, every second of my life. I didn't have to be in the deep water as I had always imagined. This notion thrilled me.

It rippled toward me, somehow blacker than the black water. It was the first time I had actually seen it. It was made of water and completely void of lines or shapes. It created a powerful wave that pulled me forward, into the dark foamy water, away from the sandy shore.

And then The Pit twisted around my leg, harder than it ever had before. It did not feel loving like it had when I was a child. It did not caress me as it had after it had killed for me, but rather it squeezed with impossible strength. I knew this was what they all had felt in those last moments, all the ones I had made The Pit take for me.

I was happy. I was happy to feel it come back to me, to want me. I was happy to know the unyielding command of my Pit.

I made no more sounds. My head went under and I knew I would breathe no more. There was only blinding, infinite night. I was no longer cold or sad. As the slimy water rushed into my lungs, I was hopeful. Perhaps I couldn't go back to my life because I was going somewhere I was meant to be. A beautiful place The Pit created for us. We would be together and there would be no more jealousy. Where I was going there would be light. I wanted this to be true.

But as I descended, a creeping thought entered my last few moments of life. I was in pain all over my body and this made me wonder if instead of my thing, the thing that loved me, it was actually Aiden Todd, no longer pale and freckled, but now a purple bloated slug that pulled me into the darkness. Perhaps Jake and his wife Andrea, still warm and angry, were drawing me down. And maybe it was my Uncle Jeremy, slick with seaweed, a hollow skeleton in motorcycle boots, who clawed at my legs as I slipped down, further and further, into the murky, hungry maw of The Pit.

Cecil

by

Cathy Clay

Cecil
by Cathy Clay

Though intent on a few more minutes in bed, Nathalie turned over when she felt sunbeams across her back. The sounds that composed the score of her neighborhood filtered through an open window. Some young men blasted their car radios with the sounds of Motown, while others listened to the works of Duke Ellington, John Coltrane, and King Oliver.

To this set, jazz artists were more than mere musicians; they were idols. These fellows hoped to become jazz greats in their own rights. Their aspirations were not impossible. They lived in the Seventh Ward of New Orleans. They were Creole, descendants of free people of color, of African, European, and Native American ancestry. Thus, jazz was a vibrant part of their culture.

She awoke with the same thought that she had fallen asleep with, Cecil Labeau. For she had adored him since childhood, and claimed him long before he noticed her. Nathalie was now twenty years old, and Cecil was twenty-five. He was tall and while his days of track and field were behind him, he still retained the physique of an athlete. He had dark penetrating eyes, the kind that would have made deception easy, but he was honest. Like the rest of the Labeau clan, he had a café au lait complexion and raven hair.

Nathalie loved to look at him, listen to him, and feel him. Yet her admiration for him went beyond his physical endowments. She appreciated his steadfast character as well. Cecil possessed a maturity and determination that was rare for a man so young. She attributed his wise manner to his father's death when he was ten. The loss made him extremely protective of his mother and younger sister, Gisselle. He guarded them as if some treacherous adversary would steal them away at any moment.

Above all else, Cecil was passionate. Nathalie loved and feared that most. He did everything with fervor, from playing the trumpet to making love. Any worthy endeavor was sacred to him. Often his passionate nature found a twin in perfectionism. He hated mediocrity. Nathalie understood that his intensity was a genuinely natural force, and he was fated to live under its spell. He could be demanding; that was the root of most of his and Nathalie's disagreements. Nevertheless, with her cool confidence and chase-worthy aloofness, they found the peculiar groove of romance. Furthermore, she was Cecil's foremost fan.

Nathalie looked forward to Friday nights. She liked to watch her beau jam to a full house. He played so intensely. An ethereal expression would cast over his face as his fingers caressed the instrument. He appeared as though he were making love to the trumpet. No one played like him. His talent made the Labeau Sextet a fixture at Club Raven, one of the best jazz joints in New Orleans.

Daydreaming about Cecil was a rewarding prelude to seeing him. Nathalie's emotions fortified a measure more every time she saw him. She never knew she could love so fiercely, but she knew she never wanted to cease.

Realizing she had lain in bed daydreaming for over an hour, she showered quickly before her mother called her down for breakfast. Cecil was coming over before he went to rehearsal, and she wanted to look her best. She was sitting at her dresser embellishing her face, when her mother came to her room.

"Sweetie, come downstairs. Cecil just drove up, and breakfast is ready."

Nathalie twirled in front of the mirror before rushing downstairs. She went to the door and unhooked the screen. The closer Cecil came, the more her heart felt like it was going to plunge into her stomach. He was wearing khaki pants and a tight white t-shirt that subtly defined his muscular torso. There is no way for him not to be vain, he just knows how not to flaunt it, she thought.

He approached the door, and kissed her on her cheek. "Good morning, Doll."

"Hi. Mama made breakfast."

"Good morning, Mrs. Volant," Cecil said, hugging her mother.

"Hello, Mr. Labeau," she patted his face affectionately. "There's more on the stove if y'all want seconds." She closed the shutters and left the room.

Nathalie sat in the chair Cecil held out before seating himself by her side. She tilted her head towards him awaiting his fingers to tousle her dark hair, and they did. She wore large gold hoop earrings, because he had once remarked that they made her look like a gypsy woman. The pearl-colored sheath dress was carefully chosen to accentuate her Coke-bottle figure. Still, she was careful not to be overtly seductive, or brazen as her mother called it; for Nathalie was well aware that it was her reserved demeanor that mystified Cecil.

She recalled an occasion when he said she did not confess love to him often enough. She batted her soulful brown eyes a few times, and waited until she had him hooked before she leaned into his ear and whispered, "Every time we're together, just know that I'm with whom I can't live without." He never raised the subject again.

73

He took her hand in his and gave her a kiss on the lips. "I love you, Doll."

"And I you." She grinned and sipped some juice. "I'm so excited about tonight."

"So am I. Ought to be standing room only." He sprinkled salt and pepper on his eggs before forking up a huge bite. "I could certainly use the money. Cause next year, this time, I'll have a wife and be starting my own club."

"I can hardly wait to be Mrs. Labeau." Nathalie fed him a strip of bacon.

"Doll, I'm ready for you to be none other."

"Then we can have a houseful of fine babies."

"Or, we might have two."

"Two?"

"Yes, a girl and a boy. That's all we need to further our line. One to have them, and one to make them."

"Well, Sir!"

"Besides, you're one fine thing. I'd prefer to keep you this way for as long as I can."

"Now you're talking like a man."

"It's the only way I know, Doll." Cecil glanced at his watch. "I'd better get to rehearsal."

"I figured I couldn't keep you to myself for long."

He flashed a cocky grin. "Baby, you know I'm yours even when we're apart. You also know that work comes before success."

Nathalie stood to run her fingers over Cecil's hair from his temples to the nape of his neck. "Give me love, my mean go-getter." They kissed and he lingered to inhale the scent of her powder. "Gisselle and I will be there by eleven."

"Okay, Doll."

~

Nathalie primped for hours and not in vain. She wore a long black backless dress that was Cecil's favorite. She stood before the mirror brushing her hair when Gisselle entered her room.

"Girl, no wonder my brother is so in love with you."

"He'd better love me because I would hate to be in this frenzy all by myself." Nathalie fingered a ruffle near petite Gisselle's bare shoulder that was slightly fairer than Cecil's. We could pass for sisters, she contemplated. Gisselle wore her wavy hair short. Delicate features and childlike dimpled cheeks made the almost twenty-one year old woman appear not to be a moment past sixteen and equally vulnerable. Cecil often had to rescue her from foolish mistakes. As a child she was inclined to break glass, play with fire, and fall in ditches. As a woman she was prone to much worse. "Might I add that you look very pretty too, my future sister-in-law?"

"Thank you, Ma'am."

Nathalie spun around and checked her rearview one last time. "Girl, we'd better go. I'm ready to hear my man." She and Gisselle grabbed their evening bags and left for Club Raven.

~

With the top down on Nathalie's black Ford Galaxie, she succumbed to the cool breezes of limitless possibilities. Bourbon Street was lit up and rambunctious. Seeing the thrill seekers wander about the Vieux Carré roused memories of when she was little and her father would take her on his moonlight percussionist gigs. She enjoyed his performances as much as she did Cecil's.

She cruised towards the edge of downtown; Club Raven was on Canal. Nathalie liked its eclectic vibe. Some went there to be seen in the latest fashions while others just appreciated good music. Though she was there to support her beau, she wanted to look good on his arm too. After all, it was hard for her not to fall under the venue's spell. It was housed in a building that had been erected prior to the Civil War; her great-grandfather was its chief architect.

Anxiously, Nathalie parallel parked then whisked out a silver compact to check her lipstick. As she anticipated, Gisselle sprang from the car and slammed the door. "Come on, glamour girl!"

Together they hurried inside. Before Nathalie knew it, she was in the spacious main hall, and sauntering under a large ruby-colored chandelier that hung from the center of the ceiling. Quickly, she glanced up to count the four smaller brass fixtures suspended from each corner of the room. According to family lore, there was one to represent each realm of the earth. With her head held high, she strode like a priestess past rows of tables covered with white cloths and crowned with votive candles.

The Fanchon Quartet had just finished playing "St. James Infirmary" when Nathalie and Gisselle arrived. They found their reserved table near the stage and seated themselves.

Nathalie was anxious to see Cecil, while Gisselle looked around for Anthony Roque.

The MC came onstage. "Ladies and gentlemen, it is my pleasure to present one of the finest jazz ensembles in New Orleans, The Labeau Sextet." The crowd applauded warmly.

Resting her elbows on the table, Nathalie leaned forward when Cecil took his place at the forefront. With the intention of blowing him a kiss, she inhaled but missed the opportunity. She was spellbound as he held his trumpet before him a few moments before raising it to his lips.

Then he blew, birthing one perfect sacred note after another as the audience swayed and clapped. Swelling with pride, she exhaled and leaned back in her chair. She understood the serious expression on Cecil's face and why his eyes stayed upon his instrument like he and the trumpet were there all alone, man and horn, a union unto themselves. Among the many faces, Nathalie eyed several well-known musicians giving strong nods of approval. She even overheard a few saying they looked forward to performing with Cecil someday. When the sextet completed "Tiger Rag" before taking intermission, she led a standing ovation.

Cecil came offstage and embraced Nathalie. He kissed Gisselle on the cheek. "Hey, there lil' sister. You're looking good tonight."

"Thank you, brother, but all praise is yours. You played like you were on a mission."

"Amen!" Nathalie pilfered a kiss from Cecil as he twirled her around. When he propped her on her feet, she locked eyes with Anthony Roque.

He stood at the back of the club taking a roll of cash from a stout man in a red suit. A tall woman clung to Anthony's shoulder. Briefly, Nathalie pondered Cecil's contemptible expression as he gazed at his old nemesis. Despite the fact that she detested everything that she knew about Roque, she forced a half smile.

Anthony Roque had spent five years in Angola for dealing heroin. Afterwards, he returned to New Orleans to resume dealing drugs and running numbers. More than a few times, Natalie had heard about how he choked a man to death in prison. From Gisselle, she learned he carried a razor and sometimes a pistol. When it came to avoiding trouble, he was as effective as a storm steering clear of rain. He would strike a woman with the same vigor he would a man, that Nathalie had witnessed. She categorized him as the worst type of thug; he had no conscience and nothing to lose.

Glee reclaimed her once she saw her beau dismissively cut his eyes across the rear of the room. She expressed gratitude with a kiss and a tight embrace.

"He has a broad hanging on him," Cecil murmured.

"Let's hope sis' doesn't notice."

"Otherwise, I'll have to --"

"Let it be."

"Alright."

Hoping to cement a merry mood, Nathalie pecked Cecil's lips again. The last thing she wanted tonight was an altercation between him and Anthony. Unfortunately, she owned a lucid recollection of their last violent encounter; the thought of it still made her cringe.

It had happened a year ago at the beach in Biloxi during the celebration of Nathalie's birthday. Gisselle and Anthony were drunk when Gisselle let her tongue slip and called him a jailbird. He retaliated by shoving her head until she was on her face and knees in the sand. Cecil intervened. After an exchange of blows, Anthony lay on his back trying to fend off Cecil, who it took three men to pull from the battle.

Nathalie feared Anthony's wounded pride would not rest and she was correct. Gisselle had confided he doled out revenge by slapping her around in Cecil's absence. Whereas Nathalie hated keeping secrets from the man she hoped to wed, she held her peace. Besides, she did not wish to further damage the sibling's now tenuous relationship.

Moreover, she was well versed on both positions. Cecil loathed his sister's choice in men, and she rebelled against him playing daddy. Nathalie also sincerely desired to be Gisselle's voice of reason. In the process, count was lost of how many times she had admonished her friend not to mistake brutishness for manliness to no avail.

"Come on, baby." Nathalie motioned Cecil to sit then eased onto his lap. She glanced around for a waitress, fearing that Gisselle might be getting antsy when she began twisting the strings of her evening bag. "How about a cocktail, Girl?"

"I'll have the same as you."

"Good." Nathalie noticed that Anthony was still flirting and hoped Gisselle would not turn around. But no sooner than she garnered the waitress's attention, her hope sank. Gisselle spotted him and almost fell over exiting her chair.

Though reluctant to rise when Cecil pinched her on the thigh, Nathalie said, "Stay here. I'll go get her."

Gisselle had hurried over to nudge the tall woman away from her man. "I thought you came here to see me."

"Ain't just you here." Anthony looked past her and blocked her hand as she tried to rest it on his shoulder. He strode toward the backdoor with Gisselle trailing after him like hot sun on bare skin.

"You always do this! You make me sick!" she said, circling him. When they came face to face, he slapped her.

Before Nathalie could do anything, Cecil rushed towards Anthony while she pled the contrary. "Baby, wait a minute! Calm down!" Despite her pleas and doomed efforts to seize his hand, Cecil grabbed his adversary, shoved him down and kicked him in the ribs several times before he regained his footing. "That's enough!" she shouted. Her heart sank as Anthony quickly steadied himself, then he and Cecil went at each other vehemently. People crowded around and Nathalie found herself a few rows removed from the locus. She moved amongst the fray, begging, "Somebody do something!" One of her heels got stuck in the groove of a plank, she stumbled, and lost her purse as she was jostled forward.

A few of the guys from Cecil's band tried to intervene, but their efforts were more verbal than physical. "Damn, Man! Why don't y'all stop?" They repeated futilely. Anthony pinned Cecil to the floor and started choking him.

Nathalie screamed, "Anthony, please get off him!"

Thank God, she thought when the bass player, Coup, came forward and grabbed Anthony by the waist. Cecil was coughing and grasping his neck as he partially rose from the floor. A small measure of relief visited Nathalie, for she began to believe the fight was over. The lighting was too dim for her to see the razor Anthony pulled from his pocket. No

80

one saw. Though Coup was still dragging Anthony, he managed to break the grip and plunge forward onto Cecil, whose neck he struck with the blade. While Nathalie sought to lock eyes with Cecil, he turned, stunned, towards her; she watched in horror as seamlessly the razor severed his throat.

As she moved closer to her beloved, the lights brightened. He was only a few feet away, yet that was the longest walk she would ever take. She knelt down, coddled Cecil's head in her lap, and stroked his hair. Gradually, his eyes closed; his face grew placid and he was gone. His blood poured onto her hands and slipped beyond her fingers like the dreams that now had escaped them both.

The room had succumbed to an eerie hush; for Nathalie it was neither eternal nor altogether transitory. Finally, someone spoke. "The law's coming," they said, fracturing the chord of silence.

Nathalie still held onto Cecil. Fritz, the pianist, had to pull her away when the coroner arrived. She wasn't resistant but rather rendered immobile. Some force within her desired to stay beside her man for fear that he may need her and leaving translated betrayal. Fritz managed to get her on her feet to escort her to his car. As they drove away, Nathalie was struck by Gisselle standing outside among the crowd groaning and convulsing; she wondered how much she genuinely mourned her brother and how much she still loved and desired his executioner.

~

The next morning Nathalie witnessed the most beautiful daybreak she had ever seen. She sat stoically upon the windowsill in her bedroom as she had done all night long. As the sun cast itself over the city in colorific phases from burnt-orange to gold, she wondered if God was trying to prove something by replacing Cecil with a pretty day. She pressed

81

her face to the glass for some semblance of normalcy or some reassurance that she was having a prolonged nightmare. However, there was a bloody dress soaking in her bathroom sink.

As Nathalie closed her eyes, she heard her mother's footfalls ascending the stairs and awaited her knock. "Come in, Mama."

"How are you, darling?"

The mere sound of her mother's voice evoked a wash of tears from an emotional reservoir of which she had not been fully aware. For a while all she could do was weep and rock in her mama's arms. "Mama, how could this happen to us?"

"Baby, I'm so sorry. I wish you didn't have to go through this. I loved Cecil, and God knows I wanted him for my son-in-law."

"How will I go on?"

"You just will, one day at a time."

"I don't see how. Let alone find what we had."

Mrs. Volant hugged Nathalie with an abiding maternal consolation. "You'll survive this, but I can't promise you'll find again what you and Cecil had. Remember, many people never find it once."

"I'm scared."

"Don't be. If you come through this, you can overcome anything." Mrs. Volant stroked Nathalie's hair. "Are you staying in today?"

"I need to . . . I'm so tired, but I can't sleep."

"Well, get in bed and I'll bring you something to eat. And don't fret about your car. I'll make arrangements to have it picked up. You just rest."

"Thank you, Mama."

Nathalie stayed in her room for two days. She mourned for Cecil and herself. She struggled to reconcile that she had to foster dreams outside of being Mrs. Cecil Labeau, bearing his children, and being the first to read and hear his music. Yet, the hardest reality for her to face was that she would never again hear him say, 'I love you, Doll.' She braced herself for the many times she would long to hear those words from him.

~

On the morning of the funeral, Nathalie awoke early, so she could cry her tears dry before the service. To her astonishment, she was unable to cry at all. Her emotions teetered from anger to numbness, yet thoughts of Cecil offered solace in between. She sought to recall as many memories as she could: his sense of humor, their togetherness, and the way he played the trumpet. Now his creed would be venerated, everybody ought to be passionate about something.

Because Nathalie did not want her grief walled off in a church, she found comfort in Cecil's mother choosing a graveside funeral. A host of people attended; among them were musicians who came to pay their respects to a fallen future great. Fortunately, as the clouds that loomed over St. Louis Cemetery No. 3 began to dissipate, so did the heavy-laden spirit of despair. Now tears and laughter coexisted during the memorial. Every now and then Nathalie caught herself smiling as one after another, relations and friends, shared reflections on Cecil.

She paid only half attention to the commentaries, and doubted that a person's genuine measure could be summed up in words. That was just like her. She then recalled Cecil once told her she was the kind of woman that had to feel something. He was right. How could any man ever understand me the way he did, she wondered.

Coup led the band in a jazz rendition of "His Eye Is on the Sparrow." The dirge stirred Nathalie's soul. The sound was more than familiar; it was the Labeau sound. She would always remember how the band's white gloves shown against the brass. Beautiful things belong together, she thought. When the band finished, Coup folded a red satin cloth longwise, and laid Cecil's trumpet on top. He went to Nathalie, and placed both in her hands.

Molly

by

Melissa Diane Algood

Molly
by Melissa Diane Algood

The neon-orange glow at the tip of the joint was all that existed.

"Get back in here, Jason!" Aaron yelled. "It's the best part of the movie! Ya know, where the baby is crawling on the ceiling!"

"You're a sick fuck. This isn't the best part of the movie."

"This isn't film theory, Lizzie." Aaron inhaled deeply, the fire on the tip of his fingers burned so bright she could see the outline of his chiseled jaw.

He brushed his long blond hair out of his eyes, and passed the joint to Lizzie. As she came down, she didn't fall flat on her face, but drifted like a feather to the bottom of the valley.

"Ugh! We're out of beer!" Maya pulled away from Jason just long enough to call from the kitchen.

"Wanna go for a ride, baby?" Aaron arched an eyebrow at Lizzie, dark eyes shining.

Jason's dad had a black BMW, perfect for an evening jaunt, so they all loaded up and headed out. Lizzie didn't know anything about cars, but this one had heated leather seats and a badass speaker system. Every thump of the bass line hit her like a hammer. So she closed her eyes and let the night wash over her, as she smoked her cigarette attempting to avoid barfing. Needless to say, this car was a vast improvement over Aaron's junker. He'd wrapped that old tin can around a light pole last winter.

"Hey, aren't the Millers in Sedona for the weekend?" Maya piped up from the backseat, like always tangled in Jason's grip.

Aaron made a sharp left toward the house, swerving onto the curb, and hit a stop sign. The pole skimmed the side of the car. They all yelled at once, and then they giggled. At last, they parked next to the brightly colored house.

Aaron used the bobby pin from Lizzie's hair to pop the lock. The four of them stumbled into the house. Maya danced around the entryway, spinning Lizzie with her. The boys went to the fridge in the garage, where they knew the beer would be.

"The - Millers - Have - A - Pool!" Lizzie stressed every word to Maya. The girls stopped spinning and ran toward the backyard with squeals of glee.

They tumbled out of their clothing, leaving on only their bras and panties. Maya dove into the pool like an Olympian. Even faced out as she was, Maya still had the grace of a ballerina.

When Lizzie dove, every molecule of water kissed her skin, every ripple felt as if she'd been taken out to sea. It seemed as if it took years for her to touch the bottom and pop back up laughing. Aaron and Jason rushed to the edge and began taking off their shoes, shirts, and pants.

"Mind if we join?" Jason asked the girls, right before cannon balling into the pool.

Drops of water shot up into the sky, a prism that glittered in the moonlight, enchanting Lizzie. The four of them floated on their backs, looking up to an unending ocean of stars.

"This water feels so...cooool," Jason whispered.

"Yeah! Beautiful." Lizzie heard her voice say, but couldn't feel her lips move.

Maya swam toward Jason. They melted into each other. Lizzie remembered the last time she was in this house. She paddled over to Aaron.

"Come on. I wanna show you something."

Somehow she was able to coax him out of the water. Maybe he eagerly followed her upstairs because she sucked on his index finger. The room was exactly as she remembered from when Mr. Miller, her coach, brought her here after practice. Midnight black silk sheets, red walls, and the massive headboard.

Lizzie couldn't stop to analyze the last time she was there. Every nerve in her body ached for the safety of Aaron. All she knew was his tongue running along her collarbone, melting her like butter. He picked her up. She wrapped her legs around his toned frame and let herself fall into the feather bed. Every touch of his lips on her skin was like an explosion.

In her sixteen years, she had no better way to explain it other than, awesome. It felt like hours that they spent tangled in those sheets, which the housekeeper had so impeccably tucked into the king size bed. When Lizzie looked at the clock, it had only been ten minutes.

"Hey bitch!" Lizzie heard the roar. "Gabby just texted me about a rave! It's in an abandoned house on 4th. Stop fucking and get down here!" Maya's voice echoed in the house.

Lizzie and Aaron redressed once they got back to the pool, where they had left their clothes. Before leaving, they raided the fridge, pantry, and medicine cabinet. Everyone hopped into the Millers' forest green Jaguar, and drove into the night, leaving behind the banged up Beemer. Through the window, Lizzie saw neon flashing lights arrayed against a black canvas sky.

That night, in the cold Arizona desert, there was house music, drugs, and a horde of teenagers crammed inside of a condemned-looking house. Lizzie took another dose of the stolen meds with the rest of them and sped up. If there was a door, none of them knocked on it. Each of them became an integral part of the mass.

Even though it was chilly, Lizzie burned, as she ran her hands over Aaron's body. She didn't just feel the music; she became the drumbeat, bass line, and guitar chord. Every drop of perspiration, flicker of light, and body movement was absorbed by Lizzie and expelled back into the group through her dancing. When she opened her eyes, sweat dripped down Aaron's forehead. His eyes were dry and bloodshot.

"Hey, let's go to the chill-out room," she suggested, pulling him close.

Lizzie directed Aaron down the hallway to the first door on the left, along with a few wayward youths. She did feel herself turn the door handle and gasp when she opened it. The entire room was soft, soundproofed, and blue.

It was long and narrow. The floor, covered in navy beanbag chairs, glowed under the black light. On the far side, across from Lizzie, *Breaking Bad* was projected onto the wall. Aaron and Lizzie weaved their way to a set of empty seats, each falling down into the most comfortable spot ever.

To her left was a couple making out. On her right another fucked against the wall. But most of the inhabitants were completely entranced with the moving images in front of them. Maya and Jason cuddled, closer to the screen.

No one acknowledged Aaron or Lizzie, even though they were hyper aware from the drugs. The tiny beads that they sat on, the padded walls, the shades of blue that bathed them, and the tenor of television all soaked into Lizzie's consciousness. The space engulfed her senses. They were all so in tune, that right on cue, the whole gathering shouted along with Jesse Pinkman, "Magnets, Bitches!"

All the lights and sounds in the sapphire abyss were calm, until Jason's nose started bleeding. "Damn, I feel weird," he whispered.

His eyes rolled to the back of his head. Maya, along with the rest of the room, were oblivious as the black light magnified the lines of red dripping from his dark eyes. His gasps blended with vibrations emanating from throughout the building.

"Hey look! Jason's dancing!" A classmate pointed to Jason's jerking body, writhing on the floor.

The group pounded their feet and clapped their hands in time with his frantic movements, until he went still. His blank face covered in blood, held no interest for them, so they turned their gaze back to the closest sparkling object.

"I wanna dance!" Maya jumped up, spun, and pulled Lizzie up from her seat.

The boys stayed behind.

What was once a kitchen and dining room had been transformed by spray paint and black lights. The DJ mixed Lana Del Rey and M.I.A., which pleased Lizzie as she was absorbed into the faction. She and Maya mirrored each other's movements. Their groins rocked, fists pumped, hips rotated, and they shook their heads so that their hair cascaded around them. The room screamed with glee.

Suddenly, Maya pulled Lizzie close, brushed a lock of hair from her face, and kissed her. Maya was soft, and tasted like a lollipop, too sweet. Lizzie tried to pull away, but Maya's arms wrapped tight around her, like a vine. Lizzie felt Maya run her hands over her back, ass, and breasts.

Lizzie wanted to forget, get lost, so they became one in time with the bass. It might have been moments, or hours, until she felt the crowd shove her, finally breaking her from Maya. Lizzie didn't hear the sirens, or know where the boys were. All she knew was the bright bubblegum pink lips in front of her.

"Run!" Lizzie heard Aaron scream beside her.

Aaron's long slender tattooed arm yanked her out of the room, through a hallway, and into the still Arizona night. She blindly followed him, but Jason wasn't with them. For a moment, Lizzie remembered seeing his body go limp on that floor. Then half the basketball team rushed past them. Lizzie giggled as the teenagers ran away, like a hive that lost their queen. Every time her sneakers pounded the pavement she felt the reverberation throughout her body. It shot like sparks into the starry sky. They ran for blocks, or miles, for what seemed like forever.

They were free.

The Match

by

Andrea Barbosa

The Match
by Andrea Barbosa

Copacabana beach, the postcard of Rio de Janeiro, Brazil, was always loaded with tourists roaming around and basking in the sun, but not today. Soccer was on everyone's agenda, everyone wanted to watch the game. Pedro moved speedily, scouring the streets like a trapped mouse inside a laboratory labyrinth. His eyes moved hurriedly and he realized, gladly, that he didn't recognize anyone. He should be in a neutral zone, or perhaps everyone else was securing a viewing place. Who would not be watching the game at this point?

From the street level, he looked up to the hills to observe the slum from whence he had descended. Staring at it from below by the beach, those little colorful wood and cardboard shacks, some made of brick and cement, littering the side of the hill, looked uninhabited, happy, friendly, peaceful even. Maybe just because today, because of the big game. But how unequivocal one could be, making such an assertion. The slum was dangerous, full of tricky, mischievous, back-stabbing individuals who would do anything to get ahead.

People walked by in haste, trying to finish their last minute shopping and errands before banks and shops closed down earlier than usual. It was an important game, after all, and who would be crazy enough not to be in front of a T.V.? This was world cup soccer in Brazil and the home team was sure to win.

The streets were in chaos, and no one noticed Pedro's ragged clothes and bare feet trying to keep up with the pace of the busy pedestrians. Easy victims, he thought. People were too busy and too preoccupied to even notice him, and he felt even more invisible. He spotted a woman, absentmindedly counting her money after stepping away from a teller machine, completely absorbed in her task, oblivious to his hunting eyes. A perfect prey. He slowed down and kept a short distance from her, observing her motions warily. She counted her money again, opened her purse and picked up her wallet. But she seemed to change her mind and instead, deposited the empty wallet back in her purse. Folding the stack of money in her hands, she cautiously inserted the notes in her jeans' front pocket, never once noticing Pedro's prying eyes on her.

Pedro ran like a hunted gazelle, jumping over flower pots and stray dogs obstructing the sidewalk, afraid the woman would soon realize her money was gone after he purposely caused her to trip over him. She had fallen on her hands and knees close enough for his swift small hands to pull the stack of notes from her pocket. In the midst of her pain and confusion, before she got up and noticed what had really happened, Pedro disappeared $100 dollars richer.

He finally stopped, breathless, on a side street, still looking from side to side to make sure there was no one following him. He was panting and needed a drink of water; his throat was dry and itchy. He needed food too. It had been…since yesterday? Yes, his last meal of stale bread had been sometime yesterday. His stomach growled loudly. He looked at the beautiful new notes now crumpled up in his small dirty hands, the money he needed to eat and drink something substantial, at least for today. And although most restaurants were also closing earlier, they would not serve a boy dressed like him. He had experienced the look of disgust from patrons and waiters alike when he had tried to enter a restaurant before. He was always sent out immediately like a pesky insect, an unwanted, unsanitary creature who didn't deserve to be there and was not worthy of being in their company or their space. How unfair it was. His mother always taught him to be respectful of people and to pray every day, but no matter how much he prayed and how respectful he was of people, he was still looked down upon, like a pest, a diseased and rabid hungry dog people were afraid of.

A street vendor was coming from the beach front with a basket full of fried seafood. On his left shoulder, the man balanced the strap of a huge white cooler which was probably loaded with soda cans. Pedro approached the man carefully, trying not to scare him, and touched his arm.

"Sir, I have money, can I have some food and a soda?" The man stopped to look at Pedro and took the opportunity to put the heavy cooler down on the ground to stretch his arm, still holding on to the food basket. He scratched his head.

"You tryin' to mess with me, little fellow? If you have any money, it must be stolen, and I don't want no stolen money," he said, looking Pedro up and down suspiciously, trying to notice if the boy was carrying some sort of gun or knife to assault him.

"Please," Pedro implored. "I'm hungry. A nice lady in the street gave me money, I was begging." He lied.

The man scratched his head again, this time removing his cap, and used the back of his hand to wipe out the sweat dripping from his forehead. "Tell you what," he said. "I'm in a hurry to catch the bus and get home before the game starts, so go ahead and take this, I'm done selling for today," he handed Pedro a paper bag full of fried shrimp. The man opened the cooler he had placed on the hot sidewalk, grabbed a can of soda, and gave it to the boy. "Now go and keep your money, let me try to catch the bus, I'm already late!" The man put his cap back on, lifted the heavy cooler and rushed off without giving Pedro time to thank him.

97

Pedro sat down on the spot, devoured the fried shrimp, and washed it down with the soda. He felt better but his stomach still hurt a little, not from hunger, but from being too full too soon. He felt like taking a nap; however, the streets were becoming too deserted. If someone was looking for him, and they probably were, he would be easy prey to catch on an empty street.

He got up shivering from the thought, felt his pocket to make sure the cash was still there, and walked towards the beach front, where he found a coconut water kiosk still open. A couple of foreign guys sat around a small screen TV by the corner drinking beer, animated with the game that had just started. It was better for him to stay around people; besides, no one would notice him with their eyes glued to the screen. He didn't move or make a sound. His life might as well be over; he was too nervous to watch it. But he knew he had to hang on till the very last hope. Everything would be fine, he thought with a hint of optimism, and then his life would move on as usual again.

It all depended on eleven men running after a ball. These critical 90 plus minutes would determine if the terror of being caught could be avoided.

What had he done? What would his mother have thought of him? She often told him to be honest. She didn't want him begging for money. She didn't want him stealing. She didn't want him lying. But most of all, she didn't want him involved with the drug gangs.

But how? How could he survive in the streets if he was just plain honest like she wanted him to be, with no food, no clothes, barely a place to sleep in that tiny cardboard shack in the slum?

And when all those other boys kept teasing him and bullying him because he was the only fool who didn't steal, didn't smoke, didn't do drugs? What kind of a slum animal was he? He tried to hang out with them, in hopes of being accepted by Maroon, the gang leader, the one who sold that stuff, something white he'd seen people sniff.

His mother had warned him to stay away from anything to sniff; it would kill him. He was afraid of it; besides, Maroon would never give it to him for free and he understood it cost a ton of money, the very money he needed to buy food and clothes, to survive. Maroon barely took notice of him, but when he did, he would kick him as if he was shooing away a stray dog, or he would spit on him.

Pedro hated Maroon. But Valdo, Maroon's right hand man, was nicer. Valdo didn't kick him or spit on him. Sometimes Valdo would even give him a slice of bread or the rest of his beer, if he was drinking one, and most of the time, he was drinking one. Although Pedro didn't like the taste of beer, it was better to accept the offer and take the last sip of the warm glass bottle than to drink the dirty tap water from his shack. Valdo treated him more like a pet, which gave Pedro an almost warm, fuzzy feeling.

Two days ago, Pedro had followed Valdo, who had been drinking more than enough beer, to the place where Maroon hid the white stuff. Valdo didn't seem to care he was being followed to the abandoned shack, the last one barely standing on the long, filthy avenue in the middle of the slum. Valdo unlocked the door, entered the shack, and lifted a ceramic tile from the broken, almost barren floor, taking from it a small clear plastic bag filled with white powder. He left the small vault open while he sat on the other side of the empty shack to sniff the substance, and Pedro saw lots of bags hidden inside. He watched while Valdo enjoyed his alcohol and drug induced stupor, and when he realized the man was too high to notice him, Pedro grabbed one of the bags, stuffed it in his pocket, and ran off.

Pedro had seen one of his neighbors buying the white stuff from Maroon many times before, so maybe he could make a deal. He came to Manuel's house with the bag and offered it to him.

"A whole bag? Where did you get that, boy?" Manuel asked, surprised.

"I need to sell it. How much can you pay me for this thing?" Pedro asked.

"I can give you three hundred. I will pay you later though, I'll get the money from the bet, tonight," Manuel said.

"Three hundred? I think it is worth more than that. What bet?" Pedro asked.

"It is worth more, sure, but I can't afford more than three hundred and I can only pay you later. I bet money on today's game, we will win, but you need to give me the bag now," Manuel said.

Pedro handed Manuel the bag and left, eager to come by later to get the money he so desperately needed.

~

Pedro was suddenly startled by effusive cheers from the guys watching the game. He had been daydreaming, thinking about how he had gotten into this mess. A goal! Had his team scored a goal? Were they winning? No! The cheers were from the tourists gathered around him. His team was losing. But there were still 45 minutes to go, though. Certainly, the team would turn it around and win. Pedro was sweating heavily, a queasy feeling took over his body, and he felt feverish. His stomach churned and he got close to the sidewalk to vomit the fried shrimp. His mouth tasted sour, but he had nothing to drink. He ran to the seaside and washed his face and mouth with the salty sea water, returning to be closer to the TV and the people for the second half of the game. He looked around, but fortunately, there was no one he knew anywhere in sight.

What would his momma think of this? Too bad she was gone. He missed her so much. No one ever found out who killed her, when she died from a stray bullet, walking home from her hourly job as a housemaid. When he found her, lying on the unpaved sidewalk, a single bullet to the side of her skull, her brains were scattered all over. The gang wars in the slum prevailed, and occasionally, a shoot-out would result in a casualty. And his mom had been one. Would he also be a casualty of the drug war if Brazil didn't win the game?

~

Before lunch time, Valdo had found him wandering in the slum. "Little traitor, you," he said, accosting Pedro. "You got the bag from the hole, didn't you?" Pedro jumped. "Maroon is furious, he wants it back," Valdo said.

"I don't have it," Pedro responded, shaking.

"Then you owe him five hundred for it," Valdo barked while holding his arm in a tight grip.

"I will get him three hundred," Pedro managed to say.

"Three hundred won't do. It is worth five hundred. He wants it tonight after the game, to celebrate the victory. And you better have it. We know where you live," Valdo said, lifting his shirt to let Pedro see a knife tucked in his pants. "You thought you would get away with it?" Valdo laughed. "You're nothing but a stray dog lost in the slum. Go get the money!"

101

Pedro looked at him in shock. Tears filled his eyes but he forced them in. "I… I'm sorry. I was hungry. I'll get the money after the game. I'll give it back to you," Pedro's voice was slow and slurred.

He got away from Valdo's tight grip and ran down away from the slum to the sunny and festive city below. He knew Maroon had many other boys in his gang. They would be looking for him to make sure he didn't disappear, that he paid Maroon back for the stolen drugs.

How could he have been such an idiot to give the bag to Manuel without payment first? What would he do now? He should have listened to his mom, but she was not there to give him a lecture anymore. There was no guarantee Manuel would pay him even if he won the bet, and he probably would not return the bag either. He knew he could not plead with Maroon. The bully would not spare him; he was furious and wanted his money back.

Cheers erupted again from the small crowd next to him. Another goal. His eyes widened. His heart was beating fast. He inspected the men now standing around him, dancing and celebrating. In a bout of desperation, he wiggled himself among them. One of the men felt a hand in his pocket and turned around abruptly, facing Pedro with disgust. The tourist yelled something in a foreign language, but before Pedro could react, the man and his friends were hitting him over the head. He barely escaped from the tourists' heavy hands, running all the way to the beach front without looking back. When he stopped to take a peek, he didn't see anyone coming after him. His head hurt and his legs were shaking. He sat near the water and reached for his pocket. It was empty. In his carelessness and fear while running away from his assailants, he lost the stolen money.

~

Rio de Janeiro woke up engulfed in a dense fog, with cloudy skies and a breeze cooler than normal. The weather was conducive to the sullen mood the locals felt after the team lost the game the day before, like the remnants of a hang-over. Such a profound sadness was hard to explain to those whose countries were not so obsessed with a World Cup soccer game. People moved about in a procession as if going to a funeral; some were gloomy, still unable to comprehend the loss. Others were infuriated, blaming the coach, the players, everything that could have gone wrong to culminate with the shameful defeat, the drama which resulted in the country's elimination from the sought after Cup. Desolation reigned. It was a tragedy, the dream was over.

The garbage man swept the street, gathering the rest of a short lived euphoria from the day before. Flags and small pieces of paper were scattered all over the place. He was upset to see so much waste. In a bad mood, he noticed a big piece of cardboard covered with crumpled newspaper sheets, a larger volume, which would require a bigger trash bin to dispose of. He approached it, and after sloppily lifting several newspaper sheets, he unveiled a gruesome scene.

A frail, brown skinned homeless boy dressed in rags, bare feet sticking in the muddy ground, lay in a pool of blood, eyes still opened wide as if he had seen a ghost. The knife that penetrated him was still visible, inserted deep into his navel. The man made the sign of the cross, covered the small body back with newspaper, and walked away, shaking his head in horror. He had seen robberies and pick-pocketing before, but had never found a dead body.

"There's a homeless beggar boy stabbed to death over there," he said anxiously to the cop stationed at the patrol booth by the beach, as he pointed to the corner where he had just found the body.

Then, picking up his sweeper, he crossed the street and resumed his tedious job.

Not This Time

by

Fern Brady

Not This Time
by Fern Brady

Javier sat on the bench and waited for the bus that would take him to work. His sagging khaki pants and zipped-up black hoodie pulled tight over his head discouraged his fellow riders from conversing with him. While *bachata* played on his IPod, he watched the *gringa* move to the farthest end of the waiting station, hugging her purse tighter. Javier shook his head, amused. He dressed like a *cholo*, but he had a good job at the Houston Zoo. True, it involved cleaning out the animals' *jaulas*, but it was an honest living.

Life in America had not been as easy as he had thought when he arrived five years ago, at the tender age of fifteen, a stowaway on a frigate. Still, he was making it. He sent what he could to his mama and little sister, Maria. One day, he'd have enough to bring them to live here, with him.

The bus pulled up. Javier waited for the other passengers to form the line to board. He liked to be last. His eye caught the political ad splayed prominently on the side of the public transport. It was the face that captured his attention. Javier had seen that face before, on a dark and rain soaked night, at the Port of Brownsville.

Vaya! Wonder if people would vote for him if they knew he was a murderer? Javier thought as he boarded.

~

"*Mi'jo*," his mama's face filled the screen of his laptop. She always got too close, not really understanding how this technology worked. "Have you finished putting together the application to that school?"

"Yes, Mama!" Javier couldn't help the exasperation. She could be such a nag. "How are you and Maria? I tried to Skype you last week, but I got no answer. I was worried."

There was a pause. His mama looked away from the camera, down at her brown-stained apron. When she finally lifted her face, there were tears in her beautiful brown eyes.

"Maria is sick, Javi," she said, holding back a sob. "I had to take her in to Aguascalientes. The doctor thinks it could be a tumor, but he says with some treatment she should be fine."

"Treatment? Tumor? How... what..." Javier felt lost. This whole time, everything he put up with, had been for the dream of bringing them to live in America. "How are you gonna pay for it, Mama?"

"The *seguro* will cover the treatments, but Javi she has a very difficult to treat type. The doctor tried to explain, but..." she looked away again.

Javier knew the Mexican socialized medical system would cover everything Maria needed up to what was available in Mexico at no cost to the family since they were entitled to the *seguro social*. But if the tumor was complicated or required treatments available only in the U.S., it would be up to the family to get the money to pay for those. And he was a long way from having the funds to bring them to live with him, let alone to pay for such expensive cancer treatments as Maria would surely require.

"Don't worry, Mama," Javier tried to sound cheerful. "We will find the money. I'll send you more this time. I'll get another job. The school thing can wait. This is more important."

"No!" Mama's eyes filled the whole screen, as she leaned in to chastise him. "You will put that application in and if you get it, we will find a way over here. This is important for you. You already made sacrifices for us. I can find a nice job in the town. I'll clean some houses, maybe help Doña Teresa with the tortilla stand. Maybe Don Ignacio might help us out and I can work off the debt. We will be fine."

"Mama, you know…"

"*Nada de eso*! You will go to school. That is the end of that."

Javier knew that tone well. When his mama got something in her head, she was as stubborn as a mule. There was no making her see sense. Anyway, she was far away and she couldn't stop him from doing what he knew he had to do.

~

"Look, Javier, I know your sister is sick and everything, but what you are planning is crazy. You are gonna end up *bien muerto*!" Emanuel ran a finger across his own neck for emphasis.

"I have to try. This guy is rich. With the money I get from him, I can buy a little farm here and pay for Maria's treatments. It's worth a try." Javier had spent several weeks planning his blackmail scheme.

"I want no part in this."

"You won't need to do anything. I'm doing all of it by myself." Javier grabbed his reluctant friend's hand and pressed the sealed package into it. "When this is over, I'm not coming back to the apartment. I'll disappear. Then you send this in to the *policía*, okay? That's all I'm asking you to do."

"Fine." Emanuel took the packet. "But if you end up dead on the news, *mano*, who is gonna help your mama and Maria then. Have you thought of that?"

~

Javier lurked in the shadows. His callused fingers rubbed the smooth surface of the photos. A shaft of dim moonlight glinted off the top one. It showed the inscription on a gold wedding band. Javier remembered the night he'd come by the object.

He'd been kneeling on the hard surface of the wooden chair, staring out the porthole of the ship that brought him to America. The crew was on leave and would be for at least two more days. The weather had been stormy as they pulled into the docks. Javier was not about to go out there and begin his new life drenched. Who would hire an immigrant stray looking like a drowned rat? No, he would just wait and hope the next night brought clear skies.

The headlights from the approaching car snapped him out of his dreams of the big four bedroom *casa* he would buy his mama when he was a rich American businessman and could bring her over. The dark, luxury sedan was turning around and backing up to the edge of the wharf. A man got out and walked to the trunk. Opening it, he dragged a rug out and pushed it up over one shoulder. In the flashes of thunder, Javier could see a limp pale arm sticking out from the rolled up carpet.

With a start, the young immigrant realized he was witnessing the disposing of a dead body, like in the old gangster movies. They really did do that here! Amazed, Javier pressed his face closer to the cold glass hopping to get a better view.

The man carried his parcel to the very edge and blithely tossed it into the dark, churning water. The fabric caught on something and the man had to bend down, struggling to release it. Finally, it fell, along with the corpse hidden in its folds, into the channel waters. The man turned and looked up, letting the rain kiss his face. Javier wondered if he thought that would clean him from the evil he had committed. Another bolt of lightning flashed as the man looked out toward the open sea. His countenance, ordinary as it was, etched itself in Javier's mind none-the-less.

Now, as he squatted in the bushes of the man's house, Javier delighted over the opportunity to finally fulfill his dreams. Sr. Gutierrez would pay, oh, yes, he would pay gladly to keep his secret hidden. He would be Maria's salvation.

Blackmail was a tricky business. If he was careful, Javier could have it made for the rest of his life. The key was not to be too greedy. He spent the last two days researching Alonzo Gutierrez. He was wealthy, but not like Bill Gates or Donald Trump. Still, a good five hundred thousand gave Javier the chance at buying some farm land and starting his own little business. With Mama and Maria to help him, they would do well, he was certain. Maria would have the treatment she needed and they would be happy together again. He would even go to school, like Mama wanted.

Of course, Emanuel would send the evidence to the police once Sr. Guttierrez paid up. It was a one-time deal. Javier couldn't let the guy get away with it, not when he had the evidence for so long. It had been a memento of his arrival, but now it belonged in the hands of the cops.

The lights in the large Memorial mansion turned off. The time had come. Once Gutierrez went up to the second floor, he would sit in his private study, while his wife slept in the huge master suite. The realtor website, HAR.com, was a wonderful resource. It had given Javier a good idea of the basic layout of the house. Even though it was not for sale right now, the archives of the previous listings included the pictures. For days now, Javier studied Gutierrez's routines, planning the best way to make his approach.

At last, the bedroom light went off and the study light clicked on. The flicker of the computer screen booting up meant Gutierrez was sitting at his big desk. Javier rose up quickly and rushed to the climbing vines decorating the walls.

Getting a firm grip he moved fluidly up to the balcony of the study and quietly pushed himself over and onto it. He stealthily turned the handle on one of the French doors. It opened for him without a sound thanks to the wad of paper he had placed there earlier in the day.

Stepping into the room, hidden behind the thick silk draperies, Javier peeked out at the killer-turned-politician. "Sr. Gutierrez," Javier spoke the name firmly, but in a low voice.

"What? Who is there?" The startled man looked around the room.

"I know what you did five years ago," Javier adapted the title of the silly movie he had watched not so long ago.

"Show yourself! Who are you? What are you talking about?" Sr. Gutierrez reached slowly toward the drawer where Javier knew he kept his pistol.

"Oh, you won't find *Pancha* there anymore, *Señor*," Javier mocked, having removed the weapon during his previous visit to the room. "Anyway, you won't need to kill me. I'm not a greedy guy. I have good evidence that you killed your wife, back in Brownsville, and you tossed her body to the sharks at the port."

"Evidence?" Sr. Guitierrez scoffed. "Those rumors have been spread by my opponents to make me look bad, but I never killed Annalise. She left me for the bum she was fucking."

"I don't think so," Javier sing-songed, thrusting a paper airplane towards the desk.

It made a smooth landing, stopping in front of Sr. Gutierrez. He'd always had great aim, Javier praised himself. The confused politician picked up the carefully constructed aircraft and unfolded the pages. The color soon drained from his face and his eyes narrowed.

"Nice pictures. What is this?" His voice was soft, controlled, as he smoothed out the wrinkles with his hand.

"Evidencía," Javier pronounced slowly, still hidden from view behind the soft fabric. "The police will have no problems matching those rug fibers. I did my homework. Your wife's grandmother had that carpet made special for her. And the ring is engraved with your and her names."

"Even if these items were to prove genuine and belonged to my ex-wife, there is no way to connect them to me." Sr. Gutierrez looked at him across the room.

Javier knew the politician could not see his face, but the coldness in those grey-green eyes made the young man shiver in his hiding place.

"There is my testimony," Javier's voice held steady despite the chilling effect of Gutierrez's glare. "I saw you take the rug out of the trunk of your car that night. Her arm was sticking out of it. I watched you throw her in the port channel to be eaten by the sharks. Then in the morning, I found these caught on a nail there. You remember don't you?

How you had to bend down and get her loose? She didn't fall all the way the first time."

There was silence now. A throbbing pulse at Sr. Gutierrez's temple was the only sign that the account of his actions had affected him.

"And, even if the police don't believe me, the press will love my story. I wonder, who would vote for you then?" Javier saw the muscles in Sr. Gutierrez's jaw clench.

"How much?"

"See, I am not greedy. Five hundred thousand and you will never see me again. You will have the items and I will disappear."

"Right. I will need time to get the money together. Perhaps in…"

"Tomorrow night," Javier was firm. "You will put the money in a black garbage bag. You will leave the bag inside the shed. Then, you will stay nice and cozy in your *casita* and, in the morning, you will find the items in the same spot waiting for you."

"Fine. It's a deal."

"*Hasta nunca, Señor.*"

~

Javier followed his new patron all day. Sr. Gutierrez had been a good boy. Javier watched him go to his bank, come out again, return home, go into his campaign headquarters, shake hands with some big wigs, and eventually return home.

114

Sitting cross-legged in the small attic space of the expensive barn-like building, Javier ate his tuna sandwich and waited. The ventilation rafter gave an excellent view of Sr. Gutierrez's house. With his nice binoculars from the zoo's gift shop, Javier kept tabs on the so-respectable *señor*.

Night fell; the sweltering Houston heat remained. Crickets began to chirp. Time wore slowly on.

Bored, Javier took his iPhone out of his pocket and began looking up nice farms or ranches for sale. Mama would want to have lots of room for her chickens and Maria, for sure, was going to want horses.

The sound of a door opening brought Javier back to alertness. Good, he thought. Sr. Gutierrez was on his way to the shed with a nice bulky black bag. The politician was dressed in a fine tuxedo. Ha! How funny to be delivering money to a poor *imigrante* in such fine attire, Javier mused.

Javier sat very still as Sr. Gutierrez lay the garbage bag of money down in the middle of the spacious building. Leaving again, Javier watched the politician return to his house.

Moments later, the elegant black Mercedes drove out of the front wrought iron fence of the mansion. No wonder he was dressed up, Javier shook his head with understanding.

Smiling, the boy climbed down from his hiding place and went over to his money. How surprised Mama was going to be when she finally got to come to America? Here they would get Maria the best treatments.

"What the…"

"Not what you were hoping for, boy?" Sr. Gutierrez's voice, from behind him, startled Javier.

Swinging around to face the politician, Javier shook the handful of shredded paper he had grasped from within the garbage bag.

"Where is my money, *señor*?"

"You ridiculous fool." Sr. Gutierrez stepped forward into a shaft of moonlight. The glint of the colt .45's silver barrel in his hand, made Javier take a step back. "Did you really think it would be that easy?"

"If you kill me, the cops will come get you."

"Please. They didn't get me when I killed her and they investigated me thoroughly. They sure as hell won't tie me to the gang shooting of a *cholo* boy."

"You don't understand, *Señor*. I took..."

The blast of the gunshot echoed for a split second in Javier's ears. His eyes widened. His body swayed. His knees crumpled, sending him face down onto the filthy floor. Maria! No...Maria! Javier's final thoughts.

~

"This is a Channel 13 Eyewitness News exclusive. Houston police arrested mayoral candidate, Alonzo Gutierrez, early this morning at his Memorial home. He has been charged with the murder of his first wife, Annalise Gutierrez, five years ago, as well as the murder of Javier Perez, whose body was found yesterday. Although the police are still investigating, Chief Alanis told reporters the authorities received evidence from Mr. Perez, which he is presumed to have mailed to police headquarters prior to his death, that links Mr. Gutierrez to his first wife's disappearance and murder. Supporters of the candidate expressed their shock and disbelief at the allegations. Susan Gutierrez, the

candidate's current wife, refused to comment. Mr. Gutierrez
will be arraigned tomorrow. We will bring you more
information on this breaking story as it becomes available. In
other news…"

The Hero

by

Bob Lynch

The Hero
by Bob Lynch

A body on the floor interrupted his perusal of the buffet options. He had just adjusted his baseball cap and squeezed tongs around an egg roll when he noticed other customers converging at a long serving cart near the one he had been considering.

He sidestepped around the sneeze guard blocking his view to see a black woman on white tile, face-down and not moving, head slightly under the buffet of unjust desserts. Dressed in a finely ironed blue Oxford and khakis, she looked like a teacher, perhaps to match the uniforms of her dear grade-schoolers. Asian servers scurried, flinging foreign words in their search for help.

Putting his plate down as he shook his head, he marveled at how trouble always seemed to find him. The woman started seizing, violently shaking, stiff as a board from head to toe. Most onlookers cleared as fast as they had come, but he calmly walked over to assist. *I got it,* he thought.

However, the Chinese manager arrived, and a middle-aged white guy dressed like a businessman was already crouched by the woman's back. He paused, knowing full well he'd get treated like just another Bubba. He stood for a moment, giving them space, but then went ahead.

The manager fumbled to turn the still-shaking lady onto her back.

Bubba could see a thick line of spittle, clear except one bright-red portion, stream from the woman's mouth and settle across a cheek, glistening like a dewy spider web to the floor.

"No, no – " directed the well-dressed man, not about to get his hands dirty. "You can't put her on her back. She might choke! Roll her on her side."

"Yeah, yeah," the manager seemed to barely get out. He did what he was told and rotated the woman back toward the floor, onto her left side.

Bubba now sat in his jeans on the floor in front of the woman, holding her as if to stop her from seizing.

The manager, still half-standing, was oddly putting his thumb below the woman's nose, like he had missed her lips trying to prevent her from biting herself. *Not a good idea*, Bubba thought. *He could lose a finger.* But Bubba figured that was up to the manager to find out for himself.

As the woman flailed, Bubba tightly gripped her upper arms and tried to cradle her head as best he could.

The other man told the manager to have someone call 9-1-1, and Bubba thought, *No one has done that yet?* The manager gibbered into the air to whoever could understand him. Workers ran back and forth down a hallway to the front desk until one brought a cordless phone.

"I need ambulance at Pandemonium Restaurant!" the manager said breathlessly. "64 Tourniquet Trel." *Tourniquet?* Bubba thought as he held the woman steady. *That's not right.*

"Turnkey Tray-el!" the manager tried again. "6-4 Turn-coat Tra-il," he said more deliberately. After a pause, the manager handed the phone to the businessman.

122

"A thirtysomething black woman has been on the floor for a couple of minutes, maybe having an epileptic seizure," the businessman said into the receiver. "Yes, she's breathing."

Each time the woman's chest rose, the businessman quickly informed the dispatcher of the rate: "Breath, breath, breath, breath, breath. She's coming to."

The woman's head started animating upward on its side, and Bubba eased his grip to quietly console her. "Is anyone here with you?"

Soon after, he piped up, hoping the manager would hear.

"She said she left her jacket in her locker," not realizing the woman didn't work there. "Can someone get it?"

The manager said, "She just came in for take-out."

With one hand still on the grown woman, Bubba used his other to type her phone number into his cell, saying, "We'll call your momma."

Before he could push the call button, the businessman called over to the woman, "Are you diabetic?" It seemed a bit brash, knowing full well Bubba was still talking to the woman. "Are you di-a-be-tic?" the businessman repeated.

Bubba continued speaking to the woman in a hushed tone.

"Shut up!" he lashed at Bubba. "I'm a trained medical professional."

"I've been overseas twice," Bubba quickly shot back, realizing that didn't come out quite how he meant it.

"I'm telling you to shut up!" ordered the man.

Bubba was taken aback, not expecting that aiding a woman in distress might end up in a fight with a stranger, so he did as instructed. He rubbed the woman's arm, letting her know things were OK while staying mum for the moment.

"The 9-1-1 operator is telling me to ask her these things," the businessman insisted, but the woman only looked up at him, eyes flitting left to right.

The businessman went back to talking on the phone, so Bubba whispered soothingly to the woman some more.

"I could drive you home," he said. "Where do you live?" Bubba clicked the buttons of his cell once more.

"Me? I'm just a bystander," the businessman said into the cordless. "No names." It seemed common not to exchange names where city and country merged and stereotypes walked the line, as if transience meant people didn't matter.

The businessman clicked off the restaurant's handset and waved it at the manager while a grey-haired white woman approached the lady on the floor.

"Are you OK?" the sweet woman asked. "We could give you a ride home."

"I've got it," Bubba interjected.

"Do you need anything, dear?" the older lady pressed on.

The businessman turned to her and said quietly and slowly, "Shut uuup." The elderly woman was surely practiced at brushing off the nonsense of such indignities over many decades. Unrattled, she stopped nonetheless.

"Thank you for caring," Bubba said. "I've got it," he reassured the senior as she gingerly stepped away.

The businessman advised having someone in the parking lot to wave in the ambulance, but the manager hesitated, torn between places to be. "You-need-to-guide-them-in," the businessman said, enunciating each word, and off the manager went.

The businessman bent down slightly and told the woman an ambulance was on its way to help.

Bubba continued to talk softly with this woman he'd never met before, until sirens announced the arrival of a rescue squad outside the Pandemonium. In came the manager and two paramedics with a stretcher on wheels.

One EMT went right to his patient, and the businessman whispered to the other, who was opening a toolbox on the gurney. The second paramedic hurriedly joined his partner, and only then did Bubba reluctantly leave the woman who would indelibly stay on his mind. He washed in the restroom and returned to the same plate he had started minutes before. At his table, joined by a companion, little time passed before he saw the paramedics roll their stretcher out to the ambulance, taking the woman to a hospital.

The manager stopped to talk with the businessman, and then he came to Bubba. "Thank you much," the manager said with a slight bow of the head. "Thank you," the manager said again.

Despite his cool demeanor, Bubba felt mildly traumatized and drained by the unexpected drama. "No problem. Is she all right?"

"Yes," the manager said. "She told paramedics she was diabetic but did not know epi-lep-sy. Thank you. Thank you." He was clearly grateful for the help.

Bubba finished his food and returned for more, solemn but subtly shaking as he re-ran events in his head. *No one even knows what I just went through,* he thought. He felt like an unsung hero, unrewarded like earlier years of military service. The world seemed to go on with little notice of what happened, but he was still affected.

Twice, a waitress checked to see if he needed a drink refill or anything else, and the second time, she laid down a bill, saying the manager took off 20 percent. *My meal was interrupted, after all.* He had wondered if he might get his whole meal for free, but he told himself it wasn't right to capitalize on another's ill fortune. This seemed a compromise.

After he paid, the manager rushed over to walk him out. Bubba was waiting for his lunch mate to catch up, anyway, so they talked standing on the curb where the ambulance had been.

"In China, we press here to stop that," the manager said, with his thumb below his nose. Suddenly, what the manager had done when the woman was shaking made sense to Bubba, although he didn't believe in it. It was a folk remedy.

"Oh..." Bubba feigned interest.

"Thank you," the manager started in once more. "You hero."

"Uh, I ain't no hero," he said to the manager outside. "We should all stop to help each other out." His dining partner came from inside, and the two ambled into the parking lot.

Bubba went back to his routine.

~

Later that day, he was at a quaint, one-bedroom house on a gravel road, surrounded by idyllic trees, hidden a bit from the other homes down the street from it. Pretty pink mums in clay pots lined the steps of its swept wooden deck, and laced white curtains with blue flowers hung in the modest front windows. It could have been the home of a single school teacher.

Bubba, sweating under the frayed rim of his rebel-flag cap, carried armfuls of valuables to a faded-red pickup that was never new to him. With gasps, he heaped each load of ill-gotten gain over the scraped, rusted tailgate and wiped perspiration with his clean backhand. Back and forth he went with his manual labor, disturbed only by a voice yelling from behind the steering wheel.

"Hurry, before she gets home!" prompted his aging momma who went everywhere with him. "It'll be dinner soon... Did you get the T.V.?"

"I got it!" he shouted back. "I got it."

Caroline Hearts Toby

by

Melissa Diane Algood

Caroline Hearts Toby
by Melissa Diane Algood

"When I saw this, I thought of you," the most perfect boy said.

My mind took me back to the first night we ever spoke, at a party, a week after I turned fourteen. It was a humid Saturday night and an ex had decided to start a fight with me. I turned into a full-fledged drama queen, and ran crying to the solace of a wooden gazebo on the edge of the woods behind the house. The tip of his long shadow touched the steps of my fortress before Toby did.

"Are you OK?" he asked.

"Yeah," I said between racking sobs.

"You want to talk?"

"Yeah." I went on for what felt like years without taking a breath. "...he's just such an asshole you know, I could do so much better than him."

"You could do a lot better... like me."

For the first time that night, I burst out laughing.

The side of his mouth turned up in a half smile. "What's funny about being my girlfriend?"

"You don't want to date me! I'm like, totally crazy."

"Maybe," his light eyes enveloped me. "But your laugh is the most beautiful sound I've ever heard."

Before I could decide if he was serious or not, a group of boys with baggy jeans, flannel shirts, and backwards baseball caps called to him, "Hey! We're leaving, man. You coming?" He stood up. The rotted wood sighed beneath his lanky frame. "I gotta go. See you around."

"See you around."

That Monday, Margo and I strolled up to the side entrance of the two story brick prison called high school, and there he was. His eyes were half closed as he sat on the steps playing an acoustic guitar the color of wheat. The scene was more fantastic than an E.E. Cummings poem.

My heart stopped beating in my chest as I followed the trajectory of his skinny left arm and the fingers of his right hand caressing the neck of his instrument. Even though he was fully clothed, a hundred feet away from me, and so into the song he didn't know I was staring at him, it was the most erotic event of my life up until that point.

Margo, my best friend since forever, nudged me. "Gawk much?"

I took a breath, not realizing I'd been holding it the entire time, and shook my head. "No way. Total waste of time. It's not as if he likes me, or whatever."

"He totally likes you, Caroline."

"How do you know? Are you psychic?"

"I have eyes." A smirk stretched over Margo's tan skin.

"Every time you speak, he looks over at you and smiles like a little kid. I'm afraid he's gonna pull on one of your pigtails during recess, or something."

My pulse sped up. "Really?"

"Watch him for yourself if you're so interested."

In class, later that day, I did. Our eyes met for the briefest of moments and it made me feel as if I'd been shot out of a cannon. I turned back to my notebook and started to write, secretly wishing my Mom would give in and buy me a cell phone.

Since I was fourteen, the best idea for expressing my undying love to him was to pass him a note after class, and that's exactly what I did. The rest of the day proved supremely agonizing.

As I walked out the front door to my bus, he stopped me, and handed me a note of his own. I wrote him a note every day for the next two years.

Now, he stood before me with the gift. I believed it was a second chance when Toby handed me a magazine with my favorite singer, Lily Allen, on the cover. It had been months since we'd spoken, but it only took me the summer to figure out I'd made a mistake by breaking up with him for a guy with a better car. But, I was too late. Toby already had a new girlfriend, Sara. Yet there he was, standing in front of me, in the alcove between our respective English classes, with the magazine I'd later cut out all the pictures from and tape above my bed.

I smiled. "Whenever I hear 'The Neighborhood,'" I think of you."

"You still like her, right?" His green eyes twinkled.

133

"Always, and forever, Toby." I hoped that he knew I was referring to him, and not the British songbird.

His smile widened and warmed my heart, "Apparently, she's coming out with a new album."

"Yeah, it's gonna be epic." That was the moment I should have told him I still loved him and wanted to have a hundred babies with him. Instead I bit my bottom lip and added, "Thanks."

"Always, and forever, Caroline." My heart skipped a beat when he said my name.

I didn't know it then, but that was the last time he'd see me, the girl he had loved a million years ago.

I went home that night and wrote a dozen love letters to Toby, as Lily Allen gazed down at me. A multitude of handwritten apologies, in various colors of ink for emphasis, explaining why I was the worst seventeen year old to breathe air. I knew putting pen to paper was archaic, but my thoughts could not be contained in a mere text. Besides it worked once before, maybe it would work again.

Even if we didn't end up behind a white picket fence, I needed him to know that I was sorry. Sorry for every dumb choice I'd made. Sorry for hurting him. Sorry for believing there was another man that could match him, much less that one existed that was superior.

For weeks I contemplated how I'd maneuver past his new girlfriend, that emo bitch, and give them to him.

Sara would often pass me in the halls in school, and call out over a horde of underclassmen. "He says I give better blow jobs, whore!" A few students laughed, but most of them continued en masse through the crowded hallway.

I'd grit my teeth and avoid her line of sight. Not *entirely* because I was afraid of her, but because I didn't want to get into a physical fight with my ex's new girlfriend. Even I was above that.

Margo turned to me. "What the fuck is wrong with that cunt?"

I shrugged. "She's totally fucking insane, like, even more than me."

"I just can't believe she says stuff like that."

"Told you, she's crazy."

Margo pushed her long dark hair behind her ears. "Besides, Sara probably has a punch card for Planned Parenthood."

"She acts like a porn star." The whole time I'd known the pixie-cut blonde she'd been more than forthcoming with every sexual act one could imagine. And although it made my stomach turn, I knew that must be the reason Toby liked her. It wasn't as if she were smarter or prettier than me, but she was sluttier.

Then, I recalled I couldn't feel too saintly, due to an evening in close proximity to a church, with Toby. To celebrate passing his driving test we drove to the most secluded part of town and I gave him a pair of oversize fuzzy dice to hang from his rear view mirror. We spent the rest of the night being the only two people in the universe. To Margo I just commented, "I mean I'm not like, perfect, but I'm not like, telling everyone about it."

Margo's dark eyes grinned. "Yeah, not *everyone*."

I punched her in the arm, then told her in a quick hushed voice, "I think I'm gonna give him the letters."

"I told you I can get Jason to give him one."

"No, I can't have my best friend's boyfriend give a guy a love letter. Besides we work together at the grill. That's too weird."

"Whatever. Then how are you going to get past her?" Margo gestured down the hall Sara had just tromped through.

"I'll meet him outside of English, or put one on his car, or something." The thought of doing any of those things seemed exceedingly desperate, but I needed him to know that if I could, I'd build a time machine.

The day before my plan would be put into motion, I pictured his big light eyes scanning the notebook paper, and the toothy grin that would be sure to follow. Cool air wrapped around me, the leaves on all the trees seemed Technicolor bright in shades of yellow, orange, and red matching my mood. The black asphalt I walked on seemed to be reflected in the overcast sky that would hover above town for months.

I didn't hear the footsteps, but a waiter from the restaurant materialized next to me, as I put the key into the door of my car.

"You're looking pretty sexy today."

I rolled my eyes at what I took as a joke, since I was still in my waitress get-up. I knew him from school, we'd even had a class together junior year. Years later, after copious amounts of alcohol had been consumed, I'd remember him staring at me in class. But I'd always thought he was harmless. Besides, at seventeen I caught a lot of guys staring at me. It was just something guys did.

He moved closer, tilted his head to the side, and smirked at me. "I had a dream about you last night, Caroline."

The way my name rolled off his tongue made the hair on the back of my neck rise. Instead of running, I asked, "Really? That's weird."

He was inches away from me. "Why?"

I laughed, then opened the car door. "Cause I never had a dream about you."

He slammed shut the door with his elbow, and leaned on it so I couldn't get to it. "You know, you're the most beautiful girl I've ever seen." He was close enough that I could feel his breath on my cheek.

Before I could respond he pulled on my long brown ponytail and tossed me to the ground. The Earth stopped rotating. I didn't feel his grip on my wrists, the pavement on the back of my head, or hear the metallic clink his belt buckle made. But I did feel when he tore me in half, as if I were no stronger than a piece of paper. In my head I was clawing, crying, and screaming, but all that came forth was a whisper. I lay in the gutter next to my car, with him on top of me, as if I'd invited him, and he hadn't just shoved me to the dirt.

After, whenever that was, I sat on the hood of my car. My arms were red and blotchy, but I didn't know if it was from him or the cold air. I drove home, raced to the bathroom, and scrubbed until my skin was raw. I didn't get out of the shower until all the hot water was gone, and Mom pounded

137

on the door because dinner was ready.

It was three days later before I told her. We were at the dinner table and I couldn't stand to stare at the pork chops and macaroni and cheese for another moment.

"Mom." I stabbed my dinner with a fork. "Something really bad happened the other day."

"What happened? Lilly Allen decide to leave the music scene?"

"No."

"Are you still upset about Toby? Maybe if you give him just one of those dozen letters you spent forever writing he'd forgive you." She threw me a grin, but it faded away when our eyes met.

"It was the worst fucking thing, ever."

I knew my tone hit her hard when she didn't reprimand me for cursing. "Tell me, Caroline."

Unable to let the word 'rape' enter our house because then it would never leave. It died on my lips. Tripping over the words, I began, "I was at the restaurant... and this guy from school... he... you know... like when I was trying to leave."

"Did he hurt you?"

My brain refused to form coherent sentences.

Her voice became darker, "What did he do?"

I looked back down to my fork and thought about how much better life would be if I felt less than an inanimate object.

"Everything."

That night she insisted we go to the ER, even if it was no longer an emergency. I was handed some pills, blood was drawn, and every opening of my body was swabbed and photographed. But, the questions were the worst because that was when I was forced to say his name. As if he deserved a name. He didn't deserve to see a sunset, have a birthday, or drink water much less to be recognized as a human being.

"We'll have to call the police and you'll have to give a statement, Caroline," the doctor said. She handed me back my clothes.

"I don't want to talk to the police." It was the first full sentence I'd said with such force since it happened.

"You're a minor, it's not up to you."

I turned to my mom, who insisted on being present for my continued humiliation. I hadn't fully appreciated her presence until I begged, "Please, don't make me talk to the cops, Mom."

The doctor moved closer to my mother. "Your daughter might not be the only one."

But I was seventeen. I didn't care about any other girls. I only knew that I could never say his name again, much less see him at court. Besides, then everyone at school would know, and it wasn't as if he didn't have more friends than me. No one would believe me over the popular jock who could get any girl he wanted.

Years later, I'd wonder if it would have been better if I had testified, and he ended up in jail, even if it was only juvie. I just couldn't handle being crucified during my senior year along with actually being a teenager.

The next day my mother insisted that we go to my boss, at the very least. When all three of us sat down in his office above the bustling bar and grill, I felt as if the room was shrinking in on me. The only way I could get it to stop was to pretend I was back in that gazebo with Toby. I looked across the desk littered with papers, pretended he was my first love, and we were talking about music, not that a guy we both knew had raped me. I told the whole story, sparing no detail, at least up until the doctor.

The middle aged overweight man reverted to himself when he turned from me toward my mom and asked, "Would it be all right if we spoke about this alone ma'am."

She nodded and I was sent to sit outside. As if their conversation didn't concern me or might hurt me further when nothing more could hurt me since I'd become a shell of a person. Sensory overload caused me to shut down. I never realized how flimsy his office door was until I heard the conversation.

My mother started. "So, what do you plan on doing about this? Fire him I presume?"

"Well, I'd have to talk to him first..."

"Why?"

"There are two sides to every story, ma'am."

"Are you accusing my daughter of lying about being raped by one of her co-workers?"

"No." He coughed. "Not saying that at all. It's just that there are channels we have to go through before anything can be done."

"What channels?"

"Well first I'll bring him and his parents in. I've known them for years. His mother is the head chef. I need to talk to her once we're done here."

I almost smiled when I heard my mother's voice turn into the hiss of a viper. "*When we're done here?* Is that what you'd want someone to say to you if *your* daughter had just been attacked?"

"No." He coughed again, louder. "It's just that it's going to be her word against his, I mean, she destroyed all the evidence."

"You're telling me she's a liar because she took a shower after some animal..." But my mother didn't continue. She didn't need to. After all my boss didn't feel Satan's fingers tugging at his underwear, a tongue on his collarbone, or taste a sweaty palm when Satan covered his mouth so he could finished.

"She's so young ma'am, maybe she got confused."

My mother rushed out of the room, pulled me out of the chair, and dragged me to the car. I'd been electrocuted by his words.

It was as simple as: a teenage girl simply couldn't be trusted. The sedan pealed out, and without looking at me, my mother growled, "You're never going back there, Caroline."

My heart restarted. "Fuck that. I didn't do anything wrong, Mom."

"I know that, but they don't. Do you really want to work with someone who thinks you're lying? Someone who thinks some kid is above assault just because he knows his mother?"

"If I don't go back, then he won."

"No, he didn't."

"I can't believe this shit..."

"You aren't going back, ever. And stop cursing so fucking much, Caroline."

There was nothing between us until we pulled into the driveway and I said. "I love you, Mommy."

She turned to me, her dark eyes a monsoon of tears. "I love you too, baby."

The next few weeks of school were particularly annoying, mainly because I was forced to be conscious for such an extended period of time. If I wasn't doodling on all of my papers then I had my head on my desk blocking out the world. I didn't think my actions were too far from the norm until my English teacher held me after class.

"Caroline, you haven't turned in your term paper."

I stared at the mustard stain on Mrs. Jennings' blouse until I remembered what book I was supposed to read. "I haven't finished it yet. I'll get it to you on Monday."

"It was due yesterday, and *Of Mice and Men* is only one hundred and seven pages."

"I've just been really busy."

She smiled and I saw wine colored lipstick on her teeth. "I know that seniors like to party, but usually you're tearing through books left and right. Now you're either asleep or daydreaming. What's going on with you, Caroline?"

For some reason a fire ignited in me and fury overtook my body. "My life just sucks, so feel free to fail me, or whatever." I turned and walked toward the door.

"We're not done talking!" She called after me, but I was already on Saturn.

"So there's this show on Friday that Jason can't go to because he has to pick up after someone that quit." Margo stared at me as if she were attempting to look through me. "So since I know you're free, wanna be my date?" she speared her salad and shoved the leafy greens into her mouth.

"Maybe." I shrugged from across the lunch table at her.

"Are you at least gonna eat?"

I tore off a piece of the peanut butter and jelly sandwich my mom forced me to take to school, and tossed it into my mouth. "Happy?"

"That's the most I've seen you eat in weeks."

"I'm on a diet."

"Stop with the bullshit, what is up with you?"

"Nothing." The girls at the far end of the table cleared their trays and walked to the bathroom for their after lunch cigarette.

"Did you give Toby the letters yet?"

"No." It seemed like another person wrote them, even if every word was still true.

"Well you should, at least then you'd know if he still loved you."

"Whatever."

Margo's hazel eyes doubled in size. "Who are you and where is my bestie?"

"I'm right here."

"No, you're not. It's like you're a damn ghost, it's like, totally freaking me out."

"I'm fine." My voice turned into a razor I wanted to slash against her throat. "Just PMS."

She rolled her eyes. "Nice try, but that's next week. Jason told me you quit, for like no reason, and everyone at the restaurant is talking about it."

"Glad I can be entertainment for someone."

Margo leaned closer. "If you just gave him the letters, maybe you could get over him."

"I don't want to talk about Toby right now."

"See, that's what I'm talking about. He's all you've been thinking about for months, and you're just giving up, without a fight. The real Caroline would never do that."

I stood up and slung my messenger bag over my shoulder. "Maybe you just don't fucking know me then." I ate lunch in my car for the rest of the year. I couldn't bear to look at her until I learned to lock it up in a box and hide the key from myself.

The idea that anyone at the grill took notice of my absence was unsettling. I wasn't completely sure that my 'story' had been leaked to my ex co-workers and classmates until Jason came up to me at school later that day.

He stood next to me as I pulled books out of my locker. "I thought you should know what people are saying about you at the grill."

I didn't. I wanted to continue to live in disbelief, like it happened to someone else. But, curiosity got the best of me. "What?"

Jason looked me dead in the eye, as if he were diving into my soul, and crushed me. "He's saying you wanted it, but you didn't want anyone to think you're a slut, so you lied."

The only guy I'd been with was Toby. "*That's* a fucking lie," I hissed.

He moved closer to me, his voice lowered. "I know. I see the way you still look at Toby and Margo seems really concerned. I know you wouldn't have sex with that asshole." Jason attempted to pat my shoulder, but I jolted away.

"Sorry," we said in unison, but only I continued speaking as my heart pounded in my chest. "I just... you didn't tell

Margo, did you?"

His dark eyebrows furrowed. "I thought you did, but she didn't ask me about it because of girl code. You two are like, inseparable."

I turned, averting his gaze. "It's whatever." I threw my pre-cal book in my locker.

Jason's voice turned stern, as if he were my big brother about to kick someone's ass. "You should tell both of them."

"No fucking way."

"I'd want to know if you were *my* girlfriend."

"But I'm not." The reality that Toby and I were completely over hit me like a hammer. "I'm not his anything anymore. I have no right to like, talk to him, about stuff."

"You guys have a history. A lot of history. He'd be there for you, Caroline. And Margo, too, she'd want to help you."

I slammed my locker shut. "Don't ever tell a soul, Jason. Especially Toby and Margo."

"Why don't you want them to know?"

I needed to tell the truth. Just once. My words were as quick as my courage. "Because if I start telling people then *everyone* will know and think that I lied about the whole thing just to get back with Toby." And in the darkest parts of my brain I was worried Toby might think the same thing as well. "Besides it doesn't matter, it happened, I just want it to be over."

"Whatever you want." He nodded, and backed away. "You have my number if you need it."

But, I never called Jason, Margo, or Toby for that matter. I picked up the phone a thousand times, and dialed Toby's number, but I hung up before it even rang once.

Later that week, at school, I saw the devil. He strolled down the hallway with a couple of guys and stopped at his locker that happened to be a few feet from mine. Even though we were surrounded by hundreds of other kids, to me, it was only the two of us. That was until I saw Toby and Sara walking hand in hand toward me, although oblivious of my presence as they gazed at each other. The hall was so quiet I could hear my own heartbeat. I wanted to scream at the top of my lungs, punch the devil, or throw books at him. Instead I was still.

Then, he winked at me.

Again, I had the exact opposite response I'd always assumed I'd have in this situation. I raced to the nearest bathroom, and threw up everything I had eaten, ever. I didn't bother going to class because I didn't want to see Toby in the hallway. I couldn't be sure he didn't see the wink. I couldn't be sure of anything anymore.

The next few days of school, little changed. I made myself fully insulated; solitude became my reality. Toby's new girlfriend still taunted me only now I truly believed that I was a whore, a bitch, and a cunt. Normally, I would have wondered why she bothered. After all, she won. I deserved it.

All of it.

Satan took everything from me in that parking lot, including my second chance. It didn't matter if I gave Toby the letters, because I could never tell him what happened. Could never tell anyone, ever, because that just made me feel it all over again. I couldn't be *that girl*. The one so stupid she got raped.

If the experience taught me anything it was: trust no one. So, I took an empty coffee can out to the woods and burned every sweet sentence that I'd written to my first love. The curvy script that spelled out every thoughtfully chosen word would live only in my memory, along with his smell, his laugh, and unending intellect.

I saw my perfect boy in the hallway a few days after I'd burned our hopes deep in the woods of our town. Toby leaned against the brick wall surrounded by a group of what used to be my friends too. He threw me a smile, he lifted his left hand, and gently waved his fingers. A part of me found joy in the fact that I would, to him, always be the girl that he fell in love with at fourteen -- strong, daring, and sarcastic.

That was the only way that girl lived on. Instead of going up to Toby, standing on my tiptoes, and French kissing him in front of the entire senior class, I bit my bottom lip, and rushed in the opposite direction.

"Where the hell have you been?" Margo scribbled equations in pencil on our group assignment.

"Got caught up," I took the seat next to her and opened up my history textbook.

"Caroline," She tapped her eraser on my desk. "This is *physics.*"

"Oh." I closed the book, dug through my bag, and realized that I didn't have the right folder either. "Can I look off yours? I don't know what happened with mine."

"Sure," Margo adjusted the book, so I could read it as well. "What's going on? You've been acting weird for a while now."

"Nothing, I'm just tired."

"I'm your best friend, you can tell me. I'll love you no matter what."

So much of me wanted to believe her, but I couldn't bring myself to trust my only friend in the entire universe. "I just really fucking hate physics."

Her face brightened, letting me know I'd successfully acted like myself, as if we were in a play and I finally got my lines right. "I know, it's like when the fuck am I gonna use physics, in like, everyday life."

I smiled, until Margo's stare reverted to the text, and I was able to drift off to nothingness again.

When our teacher began talking, I internally recited my new mantra: *Caroline is dead, Caroline is dead, Caroline is dead, Caroline is dead, Caroline is dead, Caroline is dead.*

Then, I took a breath.

Acknowledgements

Eclectically Criminal has had a long road. It was originally scheduled to release in 2014, but, due to personal hardships within the Inklings staff, everything was put on hold. Then God took over and brought us into 2015!

With His grace and favor, we are moving forward with plans to release multiple books. Above and beyond anyone else, we at Inklings give glory to God for His guidance, favor, and grace.

Fern Brady would like to say a special word of thanks to her beloved husband, Mike, who sticks by her through thick and thin. She also wants to thank her wonderful family -- to Ramon del Villar for being willing to help bring new wind to Inklings and for always teaching her to reach for the stars; to Lourdes Del Villar for helping to make her the tenacious and independent woman she is today; and to Migs for being the best little brother ever... and enduring her during their childhood.

A special hug and kiss to the canine members of the Inklings family: Arwen, Ella, Grace, Coco, and Merlin!

Special word of gratitude to Clinica Reencuentro in San Miguel Allende. What a great place to go and learn healthy eating habits and how to manage toxic emotions. The staff there, especially Dr. Roberto Vazquez and Dr. Didi Sanchez, taught her so much and helped her find the connection to God that had somehow begun to wane.

To our readership, thanks for purchasing these books and helping make authors' dreams come true!

About Our Cover Artist

Eugene Rijn Saratorio is sole proprietor of UrBook Solutions and Beyond. He has a Bachelor of Science in Agricultural Education, majoring in Animal Husbandry. He is also a graduate of AMA Computer Learning College's course of study in Computer Systems and Networking Technologies.

His company offers services in graphic design including: book interior design, book cover design (ebook and POD), bookmarks and posters, video editing and simple animation, as well as photography with retouching and editing. Other services offered are: logo design, brand design, icons, 3D book cover, 3D presentations, and CD/DVD cases, as well as other graphic art services.

Contact Eugene at:
cyber.rijn649@gmail.com
Dropbox/box.com: Virtual.solution649@gmail.com

Facebook page:
https://www.facebook.com/UrBookSolutionsAndBeyond?ref=hl

About Our Authors

Melissa Diane Algood was born on August 13 in southern California. A proud navy brat, she moved over twelve times in her life, but has made Houston, TX her home. Her work was published in *Eclectically Carnal* by Inklings Publishing. She is currently developing a spy novel.

Andrea Barbosa is the author of *Massive Black Hole* and holds a bachelor's degree in Tourism. She took creative writing courses at Texas Tech University. She loves to travel, read, and write poetry and fiction. She maintains an Indie review blog and was a contributor on Yahoo Contributor Network and Yahoo! Voices websites. Her work has been influenced by Joyce Carol Oates, Erica Jong, Sylvia Plath, and contemporary Brazilian authors Paulo Coelho and Fernando Sabino, among others.

Fern Brady is the founder and Vice-President of Inklings Publishing. She is co-director of the Houston Writers Guild with fellow author, Denise Ditto Satterfield. She began her writing career as a foreign correspondent in Houston for the Mexico City Daily Bulletin. She taught for 15 years in Alief ISD and is a full-time Realtor in Houston. She was co-editor of Spider Road Press' *Eve Requiem* anthology. She enjoys a great life with her fabulous husband, Mike, and their three dog-babies, Arwen, Grace, and Merlin.

Cathy Clay is a native Houstonian. She earned a bachelor's degree in Creative Writing from the University of Houston and a master's in English from Texas Southern University. Her debut novel, *Agatta* was published in 2010. In addition to writing, she enjoys family, animals, and the arts.

Ramon Del Villar is a lawyer, a black belt in karate, a teacher, a private pilot, and the senior interpreter for

Houston's Federal courts. His published works include: *Payback*, a legal thriller, and *Anatomy of a Civil Lawsuit*. He also enjoys serving as President for Inklings Publishing and working with his daughter, Fern.

Meg Hafdahl was born and raised in Canada. She studied literature and creative writing at the University of Minnesota-Duluth, where she received a grant for playwriting. Her short story "Dark Things" was a recent finalist for the 2014 Jane Austen Short Story Award. Meg lives in Minnesota with her husband and two young sons. Inklings Publishing is proud to be working with her on a compilation of short stories to be released in October 2015!

Bob Lynch is a professor of developmental English and journalism at Lone Star College-North Harris in Houston, Texas. In the Army, he was an assistant provost marshal, and for many years, he was an editor at such newspapers as the *Los Angeles Times*, where he shared in a Pulitzer Prize awarded to the staff. This is his first published work of fiction, a story inspired by real events.

Thomas Mitchell grew up in the Cajun country of South Louisiana. After retiring from a technical career as an engineer/oceanographer, he turned to writing fiction and historical nonfiction. He attended the Bread Loaf Writers' Conference multiple years with his novel-in-progress, *The Levee Well,* source of this story, and a nonfiction book about oceanography and amphibious landings, *Winds, Waves, and Warriors*. He is a retired Army Reserve officer and a graduate of LSU and Texas A&M.

Purchase your copy of volume 1 in the Eclectic Writings series today!

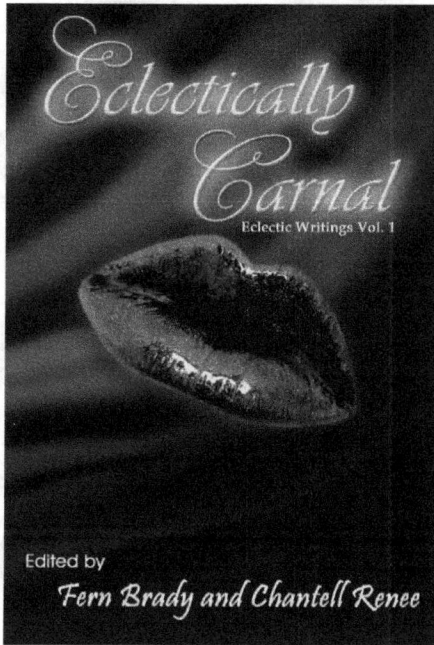

Eclectically Carnal is a collection of short stories by great authors with hot sex scenes! From a time traveling museum curator to a mythological beast cursed by evil witches, these tales will excite and titillate.

You can order directly from Inklings at www.inklingspublishing.com or purchase from Amazon. It is also in Kindle for a more discreet reading.

An international legal thriller you will find hard to put down!

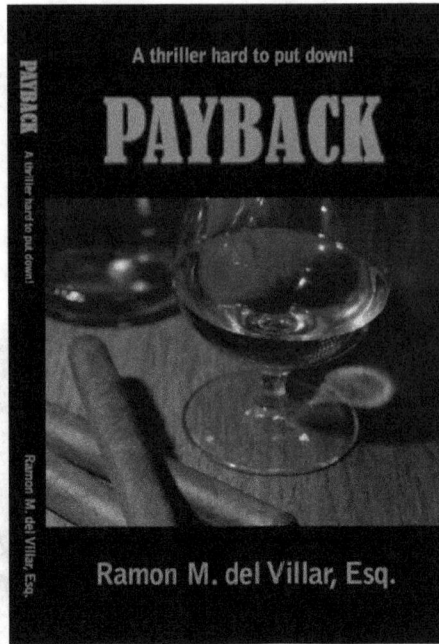

Payback is the first novel in the Roberto Duran series. Follow the intrepid attorney across the border to Mexico as he faces down drug traffickers and finds the truth behind the framing of his young client. Action packed, this legal thriller is sure to enthrall.

You can order directly from Inklings at www.inklingspublishing.com or purchase from Amazon. It is also in Kindle.

A great resource to those who want to write about civil lawsuits as well as to interpreters.